1867 And All The Rest Of It

A short, thin Canadian *history book*

By Geoffrey Corfield
Drawings by **INKBLOT**

The Publisher: **DESPUB**
2340B Clifton Street
Allanburg ON L0S 1A0

National Library of Canada Cataloguing in Publication Data

Corfield, Geoffrey, 1949-

      Canada : 1867 And All The Rest Of It / author, Geoffrey Corfield;
        Drawings by Inkblot

Includes index.
ISBN-13: 978-0-9735205-3-8
ISBN-10: 0-9735205-3-1

1. Canada -- History -- Humour.   I. Title II. Title: 1867 and all the rest.
FC173.C67 2007   971.002'07   C2006-906788-0

Editing:	David E. Scott
Illustrations:	**INKBLOT**
Cover Design:	Pat Dracup
Layout:	Tammy Nyen
Printing:	AGMV Marquis

Published without financial assistance from any agency of the federal or provincial governments.

A DESPUB publication

1867 And All The Rest Of It

A humorous look at the history of Canada: the quietest, second-biggest country in the world.

Contains only one Prime Minister and one really important date, some events you may have heard about and some you may have not, and not too many words but lots of drawings. So at the very least you can look at the pictures:

"That cannot be, there is nothing but ice there." **Sir John Ross**

"A little is precious to those that have nothing." **Montcalm**

"Sunsets are just as red as pigstyes." **Lucy Maud Montgomery**

"It needs only the nightengale." **Jacques Cartier**

"Somebody give me a beer!" **Red Hill Jr.**

"Give me a good canoe." **Grey Owl**

"Well, I guess I better start right away to become the hardy, outdoor type." **Barbara Ann Scott**

"Do not attempt to do any balancing yourself."
The Great Blondin

"Index. There is no index." **Stephen Leacock**

"These hands are clean!" **Sir John A. Macdonald**

"Ah, I did not touch it." **Crowfoot**

"You find it. They take it." **Sir Harry Oakes**

"You did not catch me." **Poundmaker**

"Good-bye to you." **Lord Beaverbrook**

"I did? I finished?" **Marilyn Bell**

"I thought I'd never see the day." **Joey Smallwood**

"One flag, one throne, one Empire." **Margaret Murray**

"One fleet, one flag, one throne." **Sir Robert Borden**

"One short, thin Canadian history book." **INKBLOT**

FROM LAKE TO POND

Failed Design for Canadian
Coat of Arms – 1867
(did not include lacrosse stick).

Table of Contents

A real-live historian speaks

Geoffrey Corfield is not a professional historian, nor a "real-live" historian, as he has called me on this page. This is all to the good because he has a fighting chance not to be greatly learned, hugely boring, and very long-winded. And happily, he's not.

Corfield knows Canada's history, but he approaches it in his very own, very quirky fashion, looking at almost every fact and social trend from a different and unusual direction -- sometimes backwards, sometimes upside down, I admit, but always right on target.

The result is delightful and fresh and, since he illustrates his text with his own wonderful small drawings, his interpretation of Canada's past will come alive for readers on every page.

1867 and All the Rest of It is a short, thin Canadian history book to look at by the fireplace when you have time to savour and enjoy good history and good humour.

J. L. Granatstein 2007

J. L. Granatstein is one of Canada's best known historians. He taught Canadian history at York University for thirty years; and has written many big, fat (and almost unread) books that can easily cover a shelf in any library (even main libraries), including *Who Killed Canadian History?* (1998),and his most recent *Whose War Is It? How Canada Can Survive in the Post-9/11 World* (January 2007). He lives in Toronto and is not ashamed to admit it.

CHAPTER ONE

Introduction

A lot of history books have been written on Canada. Mainly by historians. They cover quite a few shelves in libraries (even branch libraries).

History books are either short and thick or tall and thin. Short, thick history books sit on library shelves with their spines sticking out. Tall, thin history books sit on library shelves either on their side with their spines sticking up, or on oversized shelves with their spines sticking out.

Short, thick history books have lots of words in them, but not many pictures. Tall, thin history books have lots of pictures in them, but not many words.

This history book is different. This is a short, thin history book. It has more pictures in it than short, thick history books; and more words in it than tall, thin history books.

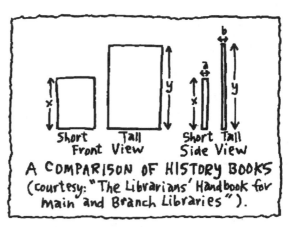

A COMPARISON OF HISTORY BOOKS (courtesy: "The Librarians' Handbook for main and Branch Libraries").

Most history books are written by historians. This one isn't. Historians are people who spend their whole lives studying, recording, documenting, reading, and writing history. Not just the day, month, and year that events occurred, but the exact time as well (3:23 p.m., 7:15 a.m., 0930 hours, half past six, four o'clock in the afternoon, that sort of thing).

This history book is different. It has dates in it, but only one really important date, and only one really important date expressed as a day, month, year. All the other dates mentioned in this history book are included as secondary dates for information purposes only, and to fulfill the obligations of The Canadian History Book Society. They have however, been provided in a form in which they can be easily disregarded or forgotten.

Historians are also serious people who write serious history books. This history book is different. This history book is serious, but only up to a point. Being too serious spoils things, including history. After all, what is history but the account of normal, everyday people muddling along through life doing mainly ordinary things, but just once in a while doing some really great things and some pretty silly things as well.

This is not the first short, thin history book in the history of history books, but it's one of the very few. The first short, thin history book was published in 1931. It had lots of drawings in it, but not nearly as many as this one. Another short, thin history book was published in 1992. But it was riddled with spelling mistakes made deliberately on purpose. This short, thin history book has no spelling mistakes in it. Or at least none made deliberately on purpose.

Most history books start at the beginning and then work forward more or less as events happened. One decade after another. Plodding through the years like a diary. This one doesn't. This history book is different.

This history book starts well past the beginning (well past the middle actually), and then presents events in chapters

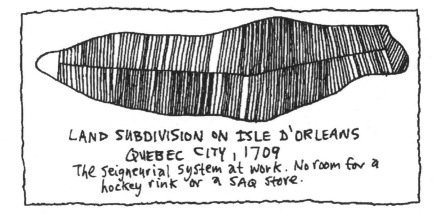

LAND SUBDIVISION ON ISLE D'ORLEANS
QUEBEC CITY, 1709
The seigneurial system at work. No room for a hockey rink or a SAQ store.

the length of which depends solely upon the number of interesting things that happened in them. If nothing interesting happened in them, the chapter is short. Also, as most interesting things in history happened in the past, this history book devotes considerably more space to this time period than to any other.

In most history books wars are important. Wars are important in this history book too. But this history book is different. In this history book wars are mentioned only if they actually happened in Canada. By eliminating all the wars not fought in Canada, and because there really haven't been all that many wars fought in Canada anyway, this history book has been able to keep its words to a minimum, allow more room for drawings, and thus attain its short, thin shape.

Most history books spend a lot of time on economics, politics, and politicians. This one doesn't. This history book is different. This history book doesn't bother with economics, hardly bothers at all with politics, and only ever mentions (briefly), one Prime Minister. The first one. After the first Prime Minister being a Prime Minister's already been done, hasn't it? So all the other Prime Ministers are just following along in the footsteps of the first Prime Minister, aren't they?

So why bother with them? Besides; economics, politics, and politicians are why short, thick history books are short and thick. And sometimes not interesting. But this is a short, thin history book. Short and thin. And interesting (you can always look at the pictures).

The Family Compact, Sir Francis Bond Head, the Reciprocity Treaty, Peter Pond, the Colonial Advocate, Rush-Bagot, the Seigneurial System, Nellie McClung, the Crow Rate, the Halibut Treaty, Rivière-du-Loup, the Château Clique, The Calgary Eye Opener, Father Brébeuf, "Ready, Aye Ready," Vimy Ridge, Dieppe, Billy Bishop, the Pork and Bean War, Louis Joseph Papineau, William Lyon Mackenzie King, the Mac-Paps, Radisson and Groseilliers, Cardinal Richelieu, Butler's Rangers, Michilimackinac, La Verendrye, the Princess Pats, and the Palliser Triangle; all have a place in Canadian history and are all fun to say. And that's why they've been mentioned here. So you can say them. All at once. One after the other.

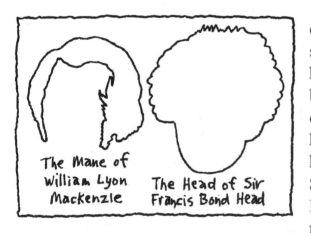

The Mane of William Lyon Mackenzie
The Head of Sir Francis Bond Head

So as you can see, from the standpoint of the history of history books, this is a different kind of history book. It has no Index, no Suggestions For Further Reading, no Dedication, no Preface, no Acknowledgements, no Foreword, no Afterword, no I-couldn't-have-done-it-without-this-list-of-all-these-other-people, no Grovelling, no Government Grants, no Bibliography, no Chronology, no Appendices, no List of Illustrations, no PhD; and only one Footnote and one Prime Minister.

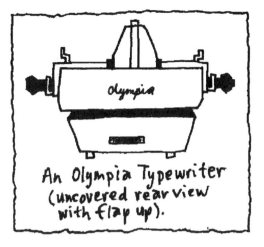

An Olympia Typewriter (uncovered rear view with flap up).

It's just a simple, short, thin history book. A short, thin Canadian history book. Not written in a university tower by an historian on a computer. Not illustrated by a computer, either. It was written in a basement by a 2B pencil and an Olympia typewriter, and illustrated by an ink pen.

A 2B Pencil Stub (semi-retired).

So this is a history book quite different from other history books. Even other short, thin history books. And certainly other short, thin Canadian history books (of which there aren't very many).

CHAPTER TWO

1867. The really important date

Unlike a lot of other countries, Canada's not cluttered up with a whole bunch of dates. There's only one really important date: 1867. If Canadians remember any date at all other than their birthday, Christmas, or when school starts, it's July 1, 1867, the date of Canadian Confederation.

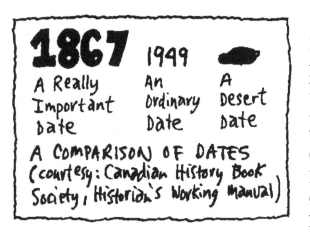

On July 1, 1867, the British Parliament passed the British North America Act and created the "Dominion of Canada." The Fathers of Confederation had thought about calling it the "Kingdom of Canada," but then one of them read out a bible verse (Psalms 72:8): "He shall have dominion also from sea to sea, and from the river until the ends of the earth;" and so they decided to call it the Dominion of Canada instead.

It's cheaper being a Dominion than a Kingdom anyway.

Being a Kingdom can be a very expensive business. You have to have a Royal Family for a start. Then you have to build them a castle and provide them with a coronation carriage and their own boat. Then there's the Royal Scandals and problems with the press that you have to put up with. No, it's really much easier just being a Dominion.

west coast

Queen Charlotte Islands

east coast Avalon Peninsula

Two Canadian "ends of the earth" (Psalms 72:8)

There are not many dominions in the world, so there are no real rules to follow to be one. You just make up your own rules as you go along. And besides, the world is already full to overflowing with republics, democratic republics, and democratic republics that aren't all that democratic at all. So they chose to call Canada a Dominion. And a very good choice it was too.

They chose to name this new Dominion "Canada" because of Jacques Cartier. Jacques Cartier from France was the first non-North American to sail up the St. Lawrence River (1535). When he got to the spot where Quebec City is now, he stopped sailing and had a chat with some of the "Indians" he "discovered" living there. (These Indians had been canoeing up and down the St. Lawrence River long before Jacques Cartier got there, but because none of them had ever canoed across the Atlantic to tell anyone in Europe about it, they were said by Cartier to have been "discovered".

The Indians told Cartier about "Kanata," a cluster of their lodge dwellings just up the river. But Cartier, being an explorer and with bigger things on his mind than just discovering a cluster of lodge dwellings, took them to mean that the entire country he had just sailed into was called "Canada." The mistake stuck. The country had a name. (Kanata is today a suburb of Ottawa.)

Unfortunately these "Indians" were also unable to convince Cartier that they weren't exactly Indians either, because Cartier wasn't actually in India as he thought. But they weren't successful with this either, and so this mistake stuck as well and they became known as Indians.

Cartier thus became the first person to use the word "Canada." And he used it quite a bit. He called this new land he had sailed into, The Province of Canada.

The name Canada first appeared on a map in 1547, and in time came to be used to designate bigger and bigger chunks of North America as more and more of it was discovered. Canada was not defined because nobody knew, least of all the map makers, just how big it really was. So they just kept on drawing it bigger and bigger and calling it all Canada.

It was quite a surprise then that when Britain took over possession of most of French North America in 1759, the name they chose to call their new territory by was not Canada at all, but the "Province of Quebec."

Although the name Canada had been overlooked and

map of Kanata from: "Where I spent my Summer Vacation", by Jacques Cartier, 1535.

given a rest for awhile, it was brought back into use in 1791 when the Province of Quebec was split up into Upper Canada (Ontario) and Lower Canada (Quebec). However in 1841 the names Upper Canada and Lower Canada disappeared themselves when they were joined back together again into the United Province of Canada, a united province with two ununited parts: Canada East (Quebec), and Canada West (Ontario). Finally in 1867 the country became the Dominion of Canada, and the Province of Canada was split up again into the provinces of Ontario and Quebec.

The Canadian Confederation of 1867 happened quietly, without a war, revolution, people throwing furniture at each other, or anything so dramatic as that. This is because Canada is a quiet country, and quiet countries don't go around making a lot of unnecessary noise and commotion.

But just because Confederation was a quiet event, it

doesn't mean that it's any less remembered. Canadians remember 1867. In fact they probably remember it too well. For a lot of Canadians seem to remember more things happening in 1867 than actually happened in it. They remember that Confederation happened when the Fathers of Confederation met around a long table in Charlottetown, Prince Edward Island in 1867 and had their picture painted.

But the Fathers of Confederation did not meet around a long table in Charlottetown in 1867 and have their picture painted. They met around a long table in Charlottetown in 1864 and had their photograph taken outside the building (most of them took their hats off except four who didn't and one who raised his hat in the air). And they met around a long table in Quebec City in 1864 and had their picture painted and their photograph taken outside the building around a small table (none of them wore a hat). And they met around a long table in London, England in 1866 and had their picture painted. But they did not meet around a long table in Charlottetown in 1867 and have their picture painted.

Silhouette of the one hat raised in the air at the Charlottetown Conference 1864. From the actual photograph (part of the arm also showing).

The dates 1864 and 1866 are therefore probably more important in Canadian history than the date 1867. But hardly anybody remembers 1864 or 1866. Canadians only remember 1867. It was in 1864 though that things really got started for 1867.

In 1864, four of the British colonies in North America -- Prince Edward Island, Nova Scotia, New Brunswick and the

United Province of Canada -- decided to get together and talk about forming a new country. They were all a bit worried about the United States. They shouldn't have been, but they were. Canada had been worried about the U.S.A. off and on since the War of 1812 ended (Canada is still worried about the

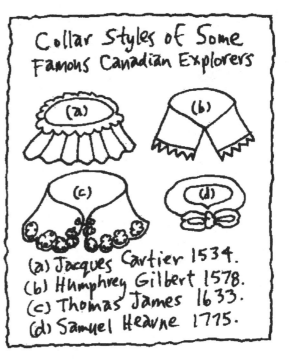

Collar Styles of Some Famous Canadian Explorers

(a)
(b)
(c)
(d)

(a) Jacques Cartier 1534.
(b) Humphrey Gilbert 1578.
(c) Thomas James 1633.
(d) Samuel Hearne 1775.

U.S.A. off and on, but for different reasons than this 1864 worrying was all about).

From 1861-1865 the United States were having their Civil War. Eighty-five years before that they'd had their Revolution.

Canada does not have civil wars or revolutions. It has rebellions or insurrections. A rebellion is something like a civil war only smaller. Much smaller. A civil war is two big parts of a country fighting each other. A rebellion is one tiny part of a country (the rebels), fighting the other much bigger part (everybody else). An insurrection is a small rebellion, sometimes called a riot or an uprising.

A revolution is a violent, sweeping change in the governing of a country, accomplished either by chopping off

The Hat Which May Have Accompanied Jacques Cartier to Canada – 1535 (ear-muffs had not yet been invented).

heads (the French Revolution), throwing tea into a harbour (the American Revolution), taking over an island (the Cuban Revolution), or shooting a Royal Family (the Russian Revolution). Canada does not have civil wars or revolutions. It's all part of being a quiet country.

Anyway, while the Americans were having their Civil War, people in Canada were nervous. They were afraid that when the war was over the Americans might just want to keep on fighting, and so turn their army around and march north instead of south and try to invade Canada again. And so these four little British colonies in Canada were worried and they decided to meet and talk about it and worry together. The United States government did not want to invade Canada again. But a group of Irish-American rebels called Fenians certainly did.

The Fenians were organized by the Fenian Brotherhood in the U.S.A. In 1866 they outfitted their own private army in Irish-green uniforms and sent them off to invade Canada. They called them "The Fenian Raids." They managed one really full-blooded raid, one quieter raid, and several threatened raids.

The Fenian's idea was that if they could conquer Canada they could hold it for ransom and swap it to Britain for Ireland. Not a bad deal, the Fenians thought. A little island with no snakes on it for half a continent full of wildlife.

Sixteen hundred Fenians in green uniforms invaded Fort

Erie and headed for Crystal Beach. Along the way they beat the Canadian militia at the Battle of Ridgeway (10 rebels and 10 Canadians killed). But four days later they had all either been captured or had shuffled-on back to Buffalo. (They never got to Crystal Beach, but today hundreds of Americans invade Crystal Beach every summer and stay until their holidays are over).

A few hundred Fenians threatened to invade Campobello Island, New Brunswick,

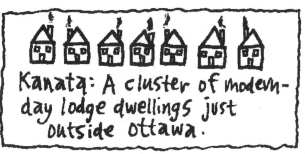

Kanata: A cluster of modern-day lodge dwellings just outside Ottawa.

but didn't. However this threat did scare the living daylights out of everybody living in New Brunswick to such an extent that New Brunswick eventually joined Confederation (in a hurry).

The Fenians gathered at the New York border south of Hemmingford, Quebec, but didn't invade. They did however invade across the Vermont border into Quebec, camp for a day, and raise their green flag on Pigeon Hill.

But with news of an advancing Canadian force they retreated back across the border and had their supplies seized and leaders arrested by the American authorities for invading without permission and camping without a permit. The U.S.A. really did not want to invade Canada again. And they didn't want anybody else invading either. Their days of invading Canada were over (they had given it quite a few good tries though).

So in 1864 these four Canadian colonies held their first meeting about Confederation in Charlottetown. The three Atlantic colonies had been thinking of getting together anyway, and the Province of Canada thought it would be a good idea if all four of them got together, so they did. They called it the Charlottetown Conference.

They chose to meet in Charlottetown because P.E.I. was the least interested of the four in getting together, and the other three thought that by meeting there it might help them persuade P.E.I. to join Canada. It didn't work. In the end, P.E.I. decided not to join Canada in 1867. They didn't join until six years later when all the others had joined without them. P.E.I. and Charlottetown were not enthusiastic supporters of Confederation.

So although Charlottetown and P.E.I. seem to most Canadians to have a strong link with Canadian Confederation (the province calls itself "The Cradle of Confederation"), they actually get more credit for the part they played in it than they really deserve. In fact while the Charlottetown Conference was going on the people of Charlottetown showed more interest in a travelling circus that was in town than they did in Canadian Confederation.

Anyway, 22 Fathers of Confederation met around a long table in Charlottetown in 1864 and had their photograph taken outside Government House around no table (24 of them appear in the photograph), and their picture painted at a ball inside Government House with no table in sight.

As they'd had a lot of fun in Charlottetown (some of them also snuck off to the circus), the Fathers of Confederation decided to meet again in Halifax, Nova Scotia. Then they had a meeting in Saint John, New Brunswick and one in

Parts of the Three Windows Appearing in the Famous Painting of the Fathers of Confederation, 1884, Destroyed 1916, Re-Painted 1965. (the rest of the windows are not visible because people are standing or sitting in front of them).

Fredericton, too. Then they decided to have another conference in Quebec City and call it the Quebec Conference. So they did. And they invited Newfoundland and Britain to come along too.

So 33 Fathers of Confederation (it was becoming popular to be a Father of Confederation by then), met around a long table in Quebec City in 1864 and had their photograph taken (30 appear in the photograph), and their picture painted (37 appear in the painting). This is the famous Fathers of Confederation painting that a lot of Canadians think depicts Charlottetown in 1867, but which is actually a combination of the Charlottetown and Quebec City delegates shown at Quebec City in 1864.

It was at the Quebec Conference that they decided that the new country would be called Canada; that it would have a federal government in Ottawa (Ottawa was already the capital of the Province of Canada), and provincial capitals in each of the new provinces; and that they would meet again in 1866 in London, England.

But P.E.I. and Newfoundland decided not to join Confederation. And New Brunswick was wavering. Without New Brunswick in Canada there would be a big gap between Quebec and Nova Scotia, and so probably Nova Scotia wouldn't join either, and so the new country wouldn't really be much of a new country after all. It would be difficult to be a "dominion also from sea to sea" if you couldn't even reach to one sea to begin with. But when the Fenians threatened to invade Campobello Island, New Brunswick suddenly decided to join Canada right-away-for-sure-where-do-we-sign?

And so the four soon-to-be-new-provinces-in-a-new-country met in London, England in 1866 to sort everything out. They called it the London Conference or the Westminster Palace Hotel Conference, depending upon if you were in the Confederation business or the hotel business. Sixteen Fathers of Confederation made the trip. They met around a long table and had their picture painted again (19 appear in this painting).

Altogether there were 36 Fathers of Confederation, the most famous of whom is Sir John A. Macdonald, the first Prime Minister of Canada, the one who went to see the Queen, and the one who opened the first parliament of the new Dominion of Canada in the brand new Parliament Buildings in Ottawa in 1867.

So although 1867 is the official date of Canadian Confederation, the dates of 1864 and 1866 are pretty important dates too. But you only need one important date for a national holiday to remember Confederation by, and July 1, 1867 is it.

Canadians always remember July 1 because it's a holiday. A day off. It used to be called "Dominion Day," but then for some reason the government changed it to "Canada Day" (1982). But Dominion Day is its real name, and it can easily be changed back (all you need to do is

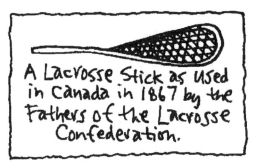

A Lacrosse Stick as used in Canada in 1867 by the Fathers of the Lacrosse Confederation.

change the government from one that wants Canada Day to one that wants Dominion Day).

By choosing July 1 as the actual day of Canadian Confederation, the British Parliament had determined that the Dominion Day holiday would always be a summer holiday. This was a good thing. A holiday in the summer is probably of more use to more people than a holiday in any other season.

But by choosing July 1, the British Parliament had also chosen a day that was very close to the already-taken American Independence Day holiday of July 4. This was perhaps not such a good thing. It meant that it would be easy for people in other countries to become confused about the two dates, the two holidays, and the two countries. The dates are just too close together. It would have made things a lot easier if Dominion Day could have been August 1 instead of July 1. But it's not. And there's no hope of ever changing it either.

So Canadians have a holiday on July 1, and the Americans have one on July 4. Some may find it confusing, but there's nothing that can be done about it now. Anyway, it's not confusing for the people who live in the two countries having a holiday three days apart.

There was something else that happened in 1867 though, other than Canadian Confederation, which also had a significant impact upon the future shape of Canada. The U.S.A. bought Alaska from Russia.

Quietly, sneakily, when no one else was looking (especially Canada which was busy putting together a new country and posing for famous photographs and paintings), the U.S.A. bought Alaska from Russia for $7.2 million in gold. Or rather, Russia begged the U.S.A. to buy Alaska, a price of $7.2 million in gold was agreed upon, and the U.S.A. paid it.

At the time a lot of Americans thought it was a real waste of money buying Alaska for $7.2 million in gold, and they called it "Seward's Folly," or "Seward's Iceberg," after American Secretary of State William Henry Seward who had negotiated the deal on behalf of the U.S.A. Now they call it "Seward's Best Bargain Buy of the Century," (two cents an acre).

How often do you get the chance to buy .01% of the world's land surface, an area twice as big as Texas and almost (but not quite) as big as Quebec, for two cents an acre? Not very often.

And so in 1867 Alaska became American, and the biggest of the four main border mistakes made along the Canada/U.S.A. border came about (none of the four are mistakes which came about in Canada's favour, which is why they are border mistakes).

The two biggest mistakes along the Canada/U.S.A. border are Alaska and Maine. Why does Alaska hang so far down into Canada? And why does Maine stick so far up? The other two smaller border mistakes are Point Roberts, Washington State, which should be in British Columbia; and the Northwest Angle of Minnesota, which should be in Ontario.

The other question about Alaska, of course, other than

why does it hang so far down, is why didn't Canada buy it? Or why didn't Britain buy it for Canada as a sort of Confederation present?

Canada didn't buy Alaska because it wasn't offered to it for sale. It didn't have the

What Canada Would Look Like With Just Two Little Canada/USA Border mistakes Corrected. Hardly Noticeable.

money to buy it anyway. Canada had just become a country in 1867, and so hadn't had the time to save up the money to buy Alaska (it couldn't even afford to bribe P.E.I. or Newfoundland into joining Confederation).

Britain didn't buy Alaska because it wasn't offered to it either. It also didn't have the money to buy it. Britain was actually trying to save money by getting rid of its North American colonies, not looking to spend money buying more (which is why it was all for Canadian Confederation).

Russia wanted to sell Alaska because it didn't have any money either. The Russian American Company was losing money in the Alaska fur trade. The Alaskan Eskimos kept attacking its settlements. Alaska was a constant bother to the Russian Czar. There were wars in Europe and Asia that were far more important to Russia than Alaska. And so Russia decided to sell Alaska. But not just to anybody. It had to be to somebody who had the money to buy it.

Russia didn't want to sell Alaska to Britain because of the Crimean War and because it knew that Britain didn't have the money to buy it. Russia didn't want to sell Alaska to Canada because that was the same thing as selling Alaska to Britain, and Russia knew that Canada didn't have the money to buy it either. But Russia knew that the U.S.A. had the money.

Russia wanted to sell Alaska to the U.S.A. because the U.S.A. had the money to buy it, and because Russia figured that the U.S.A. would one day own all of North America anyway (they certainly gave it the good old college try!).

Russia actually attempted to sell Alaska to the U.S.A. in 1853, 1856 and 1866. Finally in 1867 Russia sent a delegation to the U.S.A. with the specific purpose of selling Alaska to them. This caught the Americans by surprise. They thought that at the very best they'd be lucky to get some agreements with Russia over Alaska (fishing rights, navigation, trading oranges for snowballs). But then when Russia came right out with it and offered all of Alaska for sale to them lock-stock-and-barrel-please-take-it-off-our-hands-we-beg-you; the U.S.A. bought it the same day.

The U.S.A. bought Alaska because they had the money to buy it and because it was offered to them (desperately thrust at them is more like it, some American politicians voted for the money to buy Alaska just because they felt sorry for Russia and didn't want to offend it).

And so Canada really never had a chance to buy Alaska in the first place. It did however, buy Rupert's Land from the Hudson's Bay Company two years later for £300,000 (1869), which was really quite a super-duper bargain even by Alaskan standards. The area was much bigger (nobody really knew how big it was), and the price much smaller (thankfully Britain didn't allow the Hudson's Bay Company to offer Rupert's Land to the U.S.A.).

What Alaska Would Look Like Without That Bothersome Bit Hanging Down Into Canada (and so much easier for American school children to draw).

But in 1946 Canada paid the U.S.A. $108 million for a stretch of the Alaska Highway which passes through Canada, which makes paying $7.2 million in gold for all of Alaska 79 years before (even without a highway), look a pretty fabulous deal indeed. (The U.S.A. owes more to William Henry Seward than it does to Christopher Columbus, yet they don't have a "Seward Day," do they?)

There are two main reasons though why the Alaska-/Canada border mistake (and the Maine, Minnesota and Washington State border mistakes) turned out like they did.

Canada did not settle these border areas first and so establish squatter's rights. There was just too much other land in Canada to settle first, and too few people to do the settling. If they had done so then the border today could have looked quite different than it does.

But the biggest reason for the Canada/U.S.A. border mistakes, is that Canada relied on Britain for its border negotiating (completely for the Maine, Minnesota and Washington

State borders, and in a less than successful partnership with Britain on the Alaska border dispute); and Britain did not do such a good job negotiating Canada's borders on Canada's behalf. In fact the British did a rather poor job of it (none of the four main Canada/U.S.A. border mistakes came out in Canada's favour).

The story of Alaska starts with Russia. Russia was the first to explore the north-west coast of North America (1741). The borders of Alaska were then agreed upon between Russia and Britain (1825). It was not until 73 years later though (1898), that they were disputed between Canada and the U.S.A.

The Hudson's Bay Company were in Alaska in 1825 when Russia and Britain agreed on the borders of Alaska (Fort Yukon). But there were no Canadian settlements in Alaska. The Hudson's Bay Company were still in Alaska 43 years later when the U.S.A. bought Alaska from Russia. But there were still no Canadian settlements in Alaska.

Canada gave no thought whatsoever to Alaska or to the Alaskan border until gold was discovered in the Yukon in 1898. Then all of a sudden the Alaska/Canada border became a very important matter indeed. They didn't know where it was. So they had to find out.

The current long, straight part of the Alaska/Yukon border was set in 1825 along the 141°W longitude line. This was a pretty simple, straight-forward, no-argument border line description (it's the longest surveyed straight line in the world, 657 miles).

That part of Alaska which hangs down along the coast of British Columbia where it shouldn't, was also set in 1825. But this was not a simple, straight-forward, no-argument border line description. The southern end of the border was set as the southern end of Prince of Wales Island and the Portland Channel, 54°40'N latitude. But the written description of how to get there from the southern end of the 141°W longitude line was not very clear:

Some of the medals worn by Czar Alexander II of Russia, the man who sold Alaska.

"The boundary shall follow the summit of the mountains situated parallel to the coast, and whenever the summit of the mountains shall prove to be at a distance of more than 10 marine leagues from the ocean (34.5 miles), the limit shall be formed by a line parallel to the windings of the coast, but shall not exceed the distance of 10 marine leagues therefrom."

Can you spot the problems with this description? The Alaska/British Columbia coastline is a very rugged, jagged coastline; full of islands, mountains, peninsulas and inlets. So where do you measure "the summit of the mountains" and a "line parallel to the windings of the coast" from? Is it the first mountains you see, or the mountain range further back? Do you measure "10 marine leagues" from the tips of the peninsulas, or from the ends of the inlets? It makes a lot of difference.

Canada said it was the first mountains you see. The U.S.A. said it was the range further back. Canada said measure back from the tips of the peninsulas. The U.S.A. said measure back from the ends of the inlets. They couldn't agree. They'd had 73 years since the border description was written and 31 years since the U.S.A. bought Alaska to agree, but they hadn't thought about it. Canada had had 73 years to settle in Alaska and lay claim to its own interpretation of the border by

Some of the Fancy Furniture
Used by The Alaska Boundary
Tribunal, London, England 1903.
(the carpeting was pretty plush too)

squatter's rights, but they hadn't done anything about it. The Americans however, went into Alaska after they had bought it. And they did, after all, own Alaska to begin with. So the Alaska/Canada border dispute was heavily weighted in favour of the Americans right from the start.

In 1903 the Americans insisted that the Alaska/Canada border dispute be settled by an "impartial" (rigged) international tribunal of six "impartial" judges; three of whom would be Americans totally partial to the American position, two of whom would be Canadians totally partial to the Canadian position, and one of whom would be British whom the Americans could pressure into being totally partial to the American position. It worked. Britain suddenly realized that it did not want to upset the U.S.A. (To help Britain reach this realization the U.S.A. threatened war, sent troops to Alaska, and adopted the slogan "54-40 or Fight.") The Alaska/Canada border dispute was settled in favour of the Americans.

And so the Yukon Territory of Canada lost any hope of access to the Pacific Ocean. And Alaska would forever hang down along the coast of British Columbia where it has no business hanging down.

CHAPTER THREE

Before 1867.
A long way before 1867

Before 1867 there was no Dominion of Canada. A long, long, long way before 1867 (about 2.5 billion years ago), the Canadian Shield was formed. A long, long way before 1867 (about four million years ago), the Rocky Mountains were formed. A long way before 1867 (about one million years ago), there was ice all over the place.

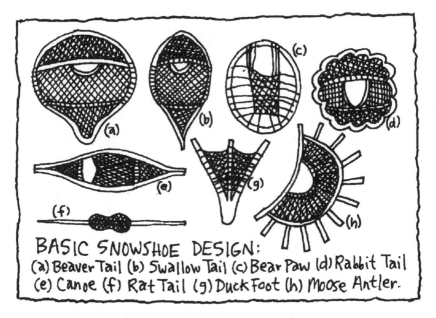

BASIC SNOWSHOE DESIGN:
(a) Beaver Tail (b) Swallow Tail (c) Bear Paw (d) Rabbit Tail
(e) Canoe (f) Rat Tail (g) Duck Foot (h) Moose Antler.

During the Ice Age all of Canada was covered with ice. Even Newfoundland and Etobicoke. The ice went west from the Yukon, through Alaska, and across the Bering Strait to Asia.

About 30,000 years ago (or about 12,000-20,000 years ago, some people say) the ice started to melt and form rivers and Hudson Bay and the Great Lakes. It was about this time as well that it's thought that people from Asia started walking east across the ice, across the Bering Strait, through Alaska, and into Canada. It is not known why they started walking east. Probably just to see what was on the other side of the ice. What they found was more ice.

Some of them went home to their own ice. But others found that they quite liked living in the ice and snow of North America and eating blubber, and so they stayed on and became Eskimos. Those that didn't much care for the ice and snow and eating blubber but didn't want to go home, stayed on but kept on walking south and east and became Indians.

Gradually as the ice melted the Indians and Eskimos spread out right across Canada. This took about 10,000 years to do. But the Indians and Eskimos didn't get along. They didn't like each other. So whenever they met up, they fought. They went looking

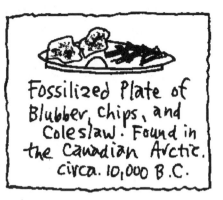

Fossilized Plate of Blubber, chips, and Coleslaw. Found in the Canadian Arctic. circa. 10,000 B.C.

for each other just so they could have a fight. And the Indians and Eskimos fought amongst themselves as well. So there was all sorts of fighting going on in Canada long before John Cabot and Jacques Cartier got here, just like there was in other parts of the world (it's still going on). The Iroquois fought the Hurons and Algonquins. The Sioux fought the Cree. The Haida fought the Bella Coola. It was just bows and arrows, tomahawks and harpoons all the time.

But in between all this fighting the Indians and Eskimos developed their own ideas about how Canada was formed. And these ideas are far more interesting than the theories that scientists have come up with about ice caps, continental drift, the Pleistocene Era, and glacial geology.

An Earth Diver plunged into the ocean, emerged with mud, and made land, animals and people. A Great Trickster stole fire, light, water, animals

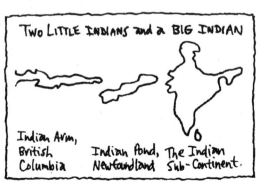

TWO LITTLE INDIANS and a BIG INDIAN

Indian Arm, British Columbia   Indian Pond, Newfoundland   The Indian Sub-Continent.

and people and created the world. Prince Edward Island was made as a pillow for a giant (they don't mention what Anticosti Island was made for).

Squash, corn and beans originated from a woman's grave. The earth was once covered with water and everything drowned except the beaver, the muskrat and the otter. The muskrat dove down into the water and retrieved a piece of earth, and from that an island grew (not P.E.I.) which became the world (not Anticosti Island, either).

A god created the world and man from a man-shaped rock. The Creator fell through a hole in the sky onto the back of a giant turtle who was also carrying the world.

These are all great, colourful, Canadian Indian stories about the formation of the world. Far more exciting and interesting than the theories that scientists have. But scientists do have their good points. One good thing about scientists is that they keep coming up with new ideas and theories. (Indian and Eskimo stories on the other hand are all handed down from the past.)

One new theory that modern-day scientists have come up with is that people came east from Asia not across the Bering Strait, but the long way across the Pacific Ocean to Mexico. Then they started migrating north. So the Canadian Indians and Eskimos were here after the Central American Indians, not before.

Another new theory is that people not only migrated to North America from the west, but from the east as well. If ice made it possible to travel east from Asia, it could also have made it possible to travel west from Europe.

They've found a very old European-looking human skull in Mexico that's as old or older than the oldest Asian-looking human skull found in North America. So it may well turn out that Europeans came to North America first from the east, even before the Indians and Eskimos came to North America from somewhere in the west.

The Grande Hermine
Jacques Cartier's Ship 1535.
(Not showing all the rigging. There's a lot of it. It's all over the place. It's a wonder they didn't all hang themselves in it before they got to Canada.)

It could be that when the Vikings, John Cabot, Jacques Cartier and the other Europeans arrived in Canada for the first time; that they were actually arriving here for the second time. It's just that the Europeans who arrived here first either didn't paddle across the Atlantic to tell anyone back home in Europe about it, and so were forgotten and forgot that they were Europeans; or else they got into fights with the Indians and Eskimos when the Indians and Eskimos arrived, came out second best and so never had the chance to be around and get "discovered" when the Europeans arrived for the second time, thus leaving the Indians and Eskimos to get all the credit for being first. At least those are the theories. We don't really know for sure.

CHAPTER FOUR

Before 1867. Less than 1,000 years before 1867

HOW THE VIKINGS SAW THE WORLD
WEST IS BEST
(no wonder they beat Christopher Columbus to North America by 500 years).

"In fourteen hundred and ninety-two, Columbus sailed the ocean blue."

But 500 years before Christopher Columbus the Vikings

had sailed the ocean blue too, and already discovered North America. It's just that they didn't stay very long and didn't write a rhyme about it[1] and so people forgot about what the Vikings had done until 1960 when the remains of one of their settlements was

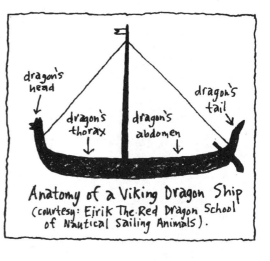

Anatomy of a Viking Dragon Ship (courtesy: Eirik The-Red Dragon School of Nautical Sailing Animals).

found on the north coast of Newfoundland.

The other thing about the Vikings of course, was that they didn't discover the U.S.A. first. They discovered Canada first (after Iceland and Greenland). Canada was discovered before the United States of America was. The Vikings found Newfoundland, Labrador, Nova Scotia, and we think (maybe) the eastern shore of the U.S.A. (perhaps). But the first part of North America that they found was definitely the Canadian part.

The Vikings were the first non-North Americans (after those who were already here), to hit the North American continent. Christopher Columbus wasn't. Christopher Columbus

---

[1] The Footnote

> *In the year one thousand and two,*
> *The Vikings sailed the ocean blue.*
> *Lief the Lucky and Eric the Red,*
> *Beat Columbus by centuries and left him for dead.*

was actually the third.

Christopher Columbus made four trips on the ocean blue between 1492 and 1504. On his first trip (1492) he discovered some islands in the Caribbean Sea. On his second trip he discovered some more islands in the Caribbean Sea. On his third trip he discovered yet more islands in the Caribbean Sea (there are lots of islands in the Caribbean Sea to discover), and the north coast of South America. But he still hadn't discovered that there was a North American continent. On his fourth trip he discovered Honduras and Panama. The North American continent. But by that time it was already 1502-1504.

The Cabot Tower, Bristol England 1897.

Five years before that (1497-1498), John Cabot discovered Newfoundland, Labrador, Nova Scotia, and (we think maybe) the east coast of the U.S.A. (perhaps, but if he did it was after Newfoundland, Labrador and Nova Scotia).

After the Vikings, the Indians, the Eskimos and anybody else who might have been in North America before them; John Cabot was the real discoverer of the North American continent, not Christopher Columbus.

Yet there is no country called Cabotia, no rivers called the Cabotia River, no province called British Cabotia, no cities in Ohio called Cabot, and no national holiday in the U.S.A. called Cabot Day. (Why is Christopher Columbus such a hero in the U.S.A. when he never even got close to it; while William Henry Seward, who was responsible for the U.S.A. obtaining Alaska, its biggest state, is forgotten except for the Seward Peninsula in Alaska? Sometimes history just isn't fair.)

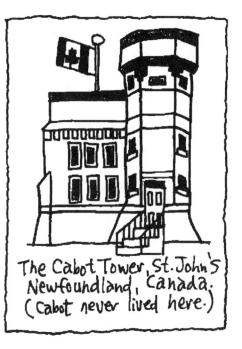

The Cabot Tower, St. John's Newfoundland, Canada. (Cabot never lived here.)

Christopher Columbus died in obscurity in Spain in 1506. John Cabot was not heard of again after 1499. John Cabot is remembered in Newfoundland and Labrador. Christopher Columbus is remembered everywhere else. Christopher Columbus is an American and world hero. John Cabot should be a Canadian and world hero. But unfortunately for John Cabot he discovered a quiet country first. The quiet top half of North America that doesn't make a fuss about heroes and changed Dominion Day to Canada Day. Sometimes history just isn't fair.

CHAPTER FIVE

Before 1867. Less than 500 years before 1867

A Tea Bag   A Fleur-de-lis
EARLY ESSENTIAL SUPPLIES
FOR EXPLORING CANADA

After John Cabot discovered North America and Britain's oldest colony of Newfoundland and Labrador, everybody started coming to Canada. Well, the French and the British did anyway (the Spanish, Dutch and Portuguese went further south where it was warmer).

The French brought the fleur-de-lis, canoeing songs, a spirit of adventure and joie-de-vivre to Canada. The British brought the Union Jack, tea, a spirit of adventure, and a poor sense of direction to Canada (all of these still exist here).

The French however, got off to the better start. They found Placentia Bay, Newfoundland and Port Royal (Annapolis Royal), Nova Scotia. And then they found the Gulf of the St. Lawrence and the St. Lawrence River. From there they discovered Quebec City, Montreal, and Lachine, Quebec; Kingston, Ontario; and the Great Lakes. From there they discovered Lake Winnipeg, James Bay (from the south), the Mississippi River, the Gulf of Mexico, Louisiana, and the New

Orleans Mardi Gras.

The British meanwhile found St. John's, Newfoundland without a lot of problems (it's almost the first place you hit due west of Ireland); but from there on in a poor sense of direction took over and they wandered off the wrong way. Where the

A Mermaid Similar To The Ones Henry Hudson Recorded Seeing in Hudson Bay in The Vicinity of "It's-A-Great-Big-Fib"Island.

French went west and south, the British went north chasing a "Northwest Passage" to China.

Thomas James headed north and found James Bay (from the north). Henry Hudson found Hudson Bay (although he didn't know it and it was the last thing he found). Martin Frobisher found Frobisher Bay. John Davis found David Strait. William Baffin found Baffin Island. Robert Bylot found Bylot Island and Cape Bylot. Luke Foxe found the Foxe Channel. All cold, frozen, northern places. The British just kept on finding cold, frozen, northern places, none of which were nearly as much fun to find as the Quebec City Winter Carnival or the New Orleans Mardi Gras were.

At first the French and the British caught fish in Canada. Then they caught animals for furs. But if the British had an initial poor sense of direction in discovering new lands in Canada that were not cold and frozen, they had a very good sense of direction in discovering new business opportunities in Canada.

MAP OF PART OF NORTH AMERICA
SHOWING IMPORTANCE OF HUDSON'S BAY, 1744.

The French Company of the Hundred Associates, and later the North West Company of Montreal, were very good at the fur trade and in discovering new territory in Canada. But in the end the Hudson's Bay Company of London, England with branch offices on Hudson's Bay and in Winnipeg, Manitoba, were better.

The North West Company sent out voyageurs with canoeing songs to paddle from Montreal to Lake Superior, pick up furs, paddle back to Montreal again, and put the furs on ships to Europe.

The British set up the Hudson's Bay Company (1670) with the exclusive use of Rupert's Land (all the lands which drained into Hudson's Bay, an area which covered Manitoba and parts of Quebec, Ontario, Saskatchewan and the Northwest Territories; although nobody at the time knew just how big

Rupert's Land really was). They then took furs by York boat (bigger than a canoe) down rivers to Hudson's Bay and from there put them on ships direct to Europe. A much more efficient way to

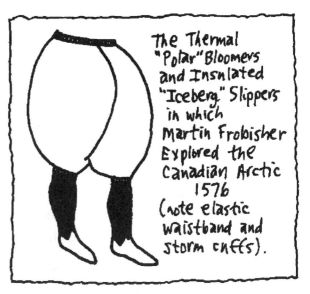

The Thermal "Polar" Bloomers and Insulated "Iceberg" Slippers in which Martin Frobisher Explored the Canadian Arctic 1576 (note elastic waistband and storm cuffs).

do business. (At one time Rupert House, Fort Albany, Fort Severn, Fort Churchill, Moose Factory and York Factory were more important places in Canada than anywhere west of Montreal.)

Eventually the Hudson's Bay Company took over the North West Company (1821). It was Canada's first corporate takeover (the Hudson's Bay Company is the world's oldest continually-trading company still in existence).

Initially the French and the British fought each other over Canada in a fur business sort of way. Then they started fighting each other over Canada in a war business sort of way too. France and Britain were always fighting each other in Europe in a war business sort of way, so fighting each other in a war business sort of way in Canada as well just seemed the natural thing to do. A war with a change of scenery. They called it "The Seven Years War."

CHAPTER SIX

Before 1867. Around 100 years before 1867

The Seven Years War between France and Britain lasted nine years in Canada. It was called the Seven Years War because it officially started in Europe in 1756, and officially ended in Europe in 1763. But in Canada, France and Britain could hardly wait to get the Seven Years War going, so they started two years earlier.

The French had Port Royal, Cape Breton Island, P.E.I., New Brunswick, Quebec and Ontario. The British had Newfoundland, James Bay, Hudson's Bay, Frobisher Bay, Davis Strait, Baffin Island, Bylot Island, Cape Bylot, the Foxe Channel, Rupert's Land, and Halifax, Nova Scotia.

The French and the British had Indian allies as well. The French had the Hurons and Algonquins (the French were first in Canada so they had first pick), and the British had the Iroquois (the French helped the Hurons and Algonquins defeat the Iroquois in 1609, so the Iroquois now hated the French as well as the Hurons and Algonquins).

So when the British came along they found a ready-made Indian ally who wanted to fight the French almost as much as they did. And the Iroquois were better fighters than the Hurons and Algonquins too. The sides were chosen. It would play a significant role in the history of Canada. The Iroquois would help the British defeat the French (Seven Years War), lose to the Americans (American Revolution), and defeat the Americans (War of 1812).

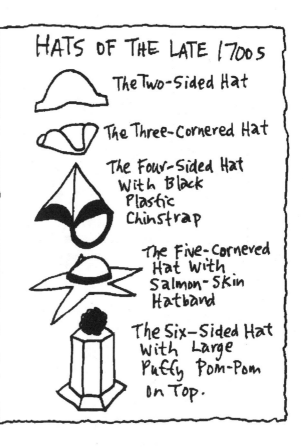

Prior to the Seven Years War when France and Britain were always fighting each other in Europe, there would usually be a little side show war going on somewhere in North America at the same time. When the war in Europe was over and a peace treaty was signed, the side show war in North America would be over as well and part of the treaty. A sort of tacked-on, side show, peace treaty clause.

In the War of the League of Augsberg (1689-1697), the British captured Port Royal, but then had to give it back under the Treaty of Ryswick.

In the War of the Spanish Succession (1702-1713), the British again captured Port Royal, but this time under the Treaty of Utrecht they got to keep it. So they changed its name to Annapolis Royal, and changed the name of the province from

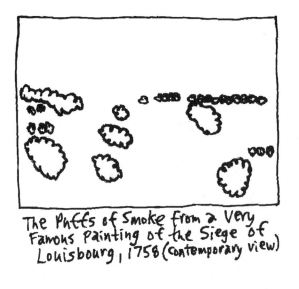

The Puffs of Smoke from a very Famous Painting of the Siege of Louisbourg, 1758 (contemporary view)

Acadia to Nova Scotia. The British also got back their Hudson's Bay forts that the French had captured.

In the War of the Austrian Succession (1743-1748), the British captured Louisbourg, Cape Breton Island, Nova Scotia; but then had to give it back under the Treaty of Aix-la-Chapelle.

But in the Seven Years War (nine years in North America), the British didn't have to give anything back to France. Under the Treaty of Paris they got to keep all of New France in North America east of the Mississippi River, except for the islands of St. Pierre and Miquelon off the coast of Newfoundland (which remain today as the last remnants of colonial France in Canada).

The biggest battle in the Seven Years War in Canada was the Battle of the Plains of Abraham at Quebec City in 1759 (the third year of the Seven Years War, fifth year of the war in Canada).

The British won the Battle of the Plains of Abraham but both country's generals, the British General Wolfe and the French General Montcalm, died gloriously in battle, became heroes, and had their pictures painted. The most famous of

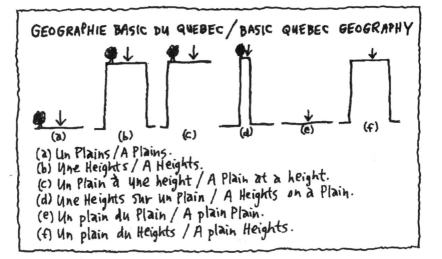

GEOGRAPHIE BASIC DU QUEBEC / BASIC QUEBEC GEOGRAPHY

(a) Un Plains / A Plains.
(b) Une Heights / A Heights.
(c) Un Plain à une height / A Plain at a height.
(d) Une Heights sur un Plain / A Heights on a Plain.
(e) Un plain du Plain / A plain Plain.
(f) Un plain du Heights / A plain Heights.

these paintings has General Wolfe dying gloriously surrounded by thirteen men including a flag bearer and an Indian sitting comfortably and staring calmly at him with his chin resting in one hand; General Wolfe dying gloriously surrounded by three men with a fourth running towards them waving a hat; and General Montcalm dying gloriously on a mattress surrounded by three Indians, a flag bearer, six other men (one of whom is looking away with his head up and one hand covering his eyes), a horse, a tent, and a palm tree.

You sometimes see the Battle of the Plains of Abraham called the Battle of the Heights of Abraham. But not by Canadians. It's Canada's battle and in Canada it's called the Battle of the Plains of Abraham. Because it was fought on a plain. Not a heights.

The battle was actually fought in a field owned by Abraham Martin (the Battle of the Fields of Martin doesn't sound nearly so romantic). The British climbed up the cliff (heights) above the Anse de Foulon (now called Wolfe's Cove) from the St. Lawrence River below, and along a path (now

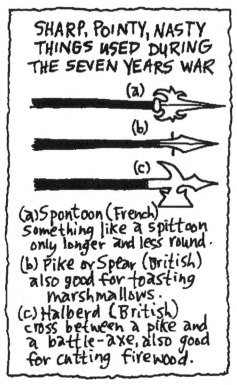

SHARP, POINTY, NASTY THINGS USED DURING THE SEVEN YEARS WAR

(a)

(b)

(c)

(a) Spontoon (French)
Something like a spittoon only longer and less round.

(b) Pike or Spear (British)
also good for toasting marshmallows.

(c) Halberd (British)
cross between a pike and a battle-axe, also good for cutting firewood.

called Wolfe's Path) to the field above. It is not known if Abraham Martin also owned the cliff, but usually in cases such as this where a steep cliff runs down to a river from a field above, a private individual does not own the cliff. The government owns the cliff and the river and a certain distance back from the river and the cliff edge for erosion protection.

Anyway, Abraham Martin was a farmer not a cliff-dweller, and the battlefield was on a plain, not a heights. The plain was on a heights, at a height; but the plain could only be said to be at a height when viewed from the river below. But the battle was not fought on the river below, it was fought on the plains above. And viewed from the plains above, the plain could only be said to be a plain, not a heights. So the Battle of the Plains of Abraham was fought on a plain, not a heights.

The next year the French regrouped at Montreal and tried to re-take Quebec. They won the Battle of Ste. Foy (1760), laid siege to Quebec City, but were forced back when the British navy arrived in the spring and saved the day.

When the Seven Years War was over (1763 in both Europe and Canada), Britain had a new province called Quebec (including all of Ontario and part of the U.S.A.), plus Newfoundland and Labrador, Nova Scotia (including New Brunswick up until 1784 and P.E.I. up until 1769 when they became separate provinces), and Rupert's Land owned by

Montcalm was lying on a mattress about here. ↓

A Palm Tree Similar to the Type That General Montcalm Died Under in a Famous Painting.

the Hudson's Bay Company (which nobody still knew how big it was).

One of the participants in the Seven Years War and the Battle of the Plains of Abraham, was Captain James Cook of the British Navy (Cook was one of a new generation of British explorers with a much better sense of direction).

Cook is a hero for discovering Australia and New Zealand (1769). But before Cook became a hero in Australia and New Zealand he was sailing

(a) ♪ (b) ♈
The hats waving in the air in the Two Famous Paintings of the Death of Wolfe.
(a) Penny 1763 (b) West 1771.

around in Canada. He was there at the fall of the French fortress of Louisbourg (1758). He helped chart the St. Lawrence River as part of the British attack on Quebec City (1759). And he mapped the island of Newfoundland (1763). The navigation skills which Cook used for discovering Australia, New Zealand, Tahiti, Hawaii and the South Pacific were learned in the cold and ice, heat and mosquitoes of Canada.

Two Palm Trees Similar To the Kind That Captain Cook was Killed Under in Hawaii 1779. (he was not killed by a falling Coconut).

The Seven Years War was the first of a series of three wars fought in Canada. The second war fought in Canada was the American Revolution (1775-1783).

The American Revolution did not actually involve Canada very much except in two instances: the American invasion of Canada at the start of the war, and the peace treaty signed at the end of the war.

When the British lost the American Revolution, under the Treaty of Paris (1783, another Treaty of Paris, Paris was a popular spot for signing treaties), a lot of the present-day eastern border between Canada and the U.S.A. was set, especially the St. Lawrence River and Great Lakes part of the border. But the complicated Quebec/New Brunswick/Maine part of the border, and the border west of Lake Superior, were still not set.

The American Revolution marked the first time that the U.S.A. tried to invade Canada. And they tried right at the start of this war. In 1775 the Americans attacked Montreal and Quebec City, and in 1776 they attacked Fort Beausejour, New Brunswick (near Sackville). They didn't get them. They did get Montreal temporarily, but they did not get Quebec City thanks to its defence by Governor Sir Guy Carleton (Carleton University) and a snowstorm. (The Americans were not very good at fighting in snowstorms, and snow helped to defeat them in the third war fought in Canada, too. In the attack on Quebec the American General Montgomery was killed, died gloriously in battle, became a hero, and had two pictures painted, none of which show any sign of a snowstorm).

THE MAINE BORDER MISTAKE
1. What the USA wanted.
2. What the border is today.
3. What Britain wanted.
4. What Canada could have had.

If the Americans had captured Montreal and Quebec City then there probably would have been no need for the third war fought in Canada, the War of 1812.

The War of 1812 was fought between Britain and Canada on the one side, and the U.S.A. on the other side. It was the Americans' biggest attempt to capture Canada.

In 1812 Britain was fighting two wars at once. One war close to home, and one war far away. The close war was the war in Europe against Napoleon (France again). It's a well-known, long war fought over a large area by big armies. The far away war was the War of 1812 in North America against the U.S.A. It's a not-very-well-known, short war fought over a large area by small armies.

The War of 1812 officially started on 18 June, 1812. In the afternoon. It lasted two years, six months, and one week. Because of this it's sometimes called the War of 1812-14. But mostly it's just called the War of 1812.

The War of 1812 started when the U.S.A. declared war

Uniform of Major-General Sir Isaac Brock showing Actual Bullet Hole.

on Britain. Officially. They didn't want to invade Britain, of course, just part of it. The Canadian part.

The War of 1812 was a war of skirmishes rather than big battles. More people were killed in one day's fighting in the war in Europe against Napoleon than participated in the whole of the War of 1812. Yet the stakes were just as high. At stake was the fate of a continent. If Napoleon had won then perhaps more of Europe would now be French. But if the U.S.A. had won then undoubtedly more of North America would now be American.

The War of 1812 produced three Canadian heroes: Laura Secord, the 38-year-old mother of five who walked 19 miles to warn the British of an American attack; Tecumseh, the Indian leader who fought with the British; and Major-General Sir Isaac Brock, the British commander in Upper Canada. The War of 1812 produced American heroes too. Even in a war which they lost and which produced few American victories, and none of any real consequence, the Americans can still find heroes.

The best-known part of the War of 1812 for Canadians is the Battle of Queenston Heights (1813). It was fought on a heights (a hill heights, not a cliff heights), and there has never been any attempt to try to rename it the Battle of Queenston Plains.

The Battle of Queenston Heights is remembered for the

British and Canadians winning the battle but losing their general. Like General Wolfe, General Brock died gloriously in battle and had

A bicycle similar to the kind it's a good thing Laura Secord didn't ride on her famous trip from Queenston, otherwise she wouldn't have got there.

his picture painted. Or rather, several pictures painted. One shows General Brock as part of an overall Queenston Heights battle scene. One shows General Brock falling and dying gloriously in a battle while charging up Queenston Heights looked upon by his men and an Indian. And another shows General Brock already fallen and dying gloriously in battle while waving his sword urging his men forward.

But for Americans the War of 1812 is even more memorable (not for their heroes or for the fact that they lost). The best known parts of the War of 1812 for Americans are: the British setting fire to Washington D.C. (1814) causing the president's house to be burned and repainted white, thus becoming known as the "White House;" the British bombardment of Baltimore causing the American flag to still be there in the morning despite bombs bursting in air, thus moving Francis Scott Key to compose the American national anthem; and the Battle of New Orleans (1815) which the Americans won, thus causing them to say that "we won the war."

But the Battle of New Orleans was fought two weeks after the War of 1812 ended. Officially. So the Battle of New Orleans really doesn't count. And under the Treaty of Ghent signed to end the war, both sides agreed to return to the same borders they had before the war began. So the declared American invasion of Canada had failed. (The Battle of New Orleans however, was more successful in moving another song writer, Johnny Horton, to compose another song, *The Ballad of the Battle of New Orleans*).

Canadians though were not just sitting around between these wars waiting for the next war to come along and the opportunity to bask in the glory of having been responsible for the White House, the American national anthem and a hit song on the hit parade. They were out there exploring and settling into the empty spaces and building their country. After all, there were a lot of empty spaces out there and up there to explore and settle into that nobody yet knew about.

Samuel Hearne (Cape Hearne) left Fort Churchill on Hudson's Bay and reached the Arctic Ocean at the mouth of the Coppermine River. Alexander Mackenzie (Mackenzie River) went north from Lake Athabaska to the Arctic Ocean by the Mackenzie River, and then went west from Lake Athabaska to the Pacific Ocean by the Bella Coola River, thus becoming the first person to cross North America by land (he arrived at Fort Chipewyan on Lake Athabasca via Montreal, New York and Scotland).

David Thompson went from Hudson's Bay to Lake Athabasca and from there down the Athabaska, Saskatchewan and Columbia Rivers to the Pacific Ocean, only to find that the Americans had got there first (the Thompson River is named after David Thompson but he was never on it).

Captain James Cook landed on Vancouver Island, but it wasn't called Vancouver Island then because Captain George

A 24-Pound War of 1812 Garrison Cannon (the field version had two big wheels instead of four little ones).

Vancouver hadn't arrived there yet. Captain George Vancouver arrived and sailed up the Pacific coast and around his island. Simon Fraser went down his river.

Joseph Brant settled the Six Nations Indian Reserve at Brantford, Ontario. Thomas Talbot settled the Talbot Tract, St. Thomas and Talbotville, Ontario. John Galt formed the Canada Company and settled the Huron Tract, Galt, Guelph, Stratford and Goderich, Ontario. Lord Selkirk had the Selkirk Grant and settled the Red River Colony (Winnipeg) and Selkirk, Manitoba. John Graves Simcoe settled York (Toronto), Yonge Street (the longest street in the world), and Lake Simcoe (not the wet part). The North West Company settled Fort William (Thunder Bay).

The United Empire Loyalists left the U.S.A. and settled along the St. Lawrence River between Montreal and Kingston (where the Lachine Canal and the Rideau Canal were built); in the Niagara Peninsula (where the Welland Canal was built); along Lake Ontario and the Bay of Quinte; and in Quebec, Nova Scotia and New Brunswick ("the most gentlemanlike province on earth").

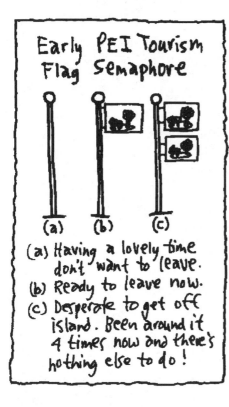

Early PEI Tourism Flag Semaphore

(a) (b) (c)

(a) Having a lovely time don't want to leave.
(b) Ready to leave now.
(c) Desperate to get off island. Been around it 4 times now and there's nothing else to do!

Not too many people settled on Prince Edward Island though because it was still quite isolated. At one time the only ferry service available to the island was provided by a little man in a boat on the New Brunswick side who took passengers across when he went out to check his lobster traps. If you wanted a ride back, you raised a flag on a flagpole especially erected for that purpose on the beach at 6 a.m. the next day. If the little man was coming out he'd flag you back. If he didn't flag you back then you had another day on P.E.I. If it was foggy or stormy, then you had another day on P.E.I. anyway.

New Brunswick and P.E.I., which used to be part of Nova Scotia, became separate provinces and P.E.I. got a new name (it used to be called Isle St. Jean). But Cape Breton Island, which used to be a separate province, became part of the province of Nova Scotia. Ontario and Quebec, which used to be together as the Province of Quebec, were separated into Upper Canada and Lower Canada (later they would be put together and separated once again).

The Canada/U.S.A. border west of Lake Superior was set as the 49th parallel as far west as the Rocky Mountains. (Most of this border just followed a straight line [the 49°N latitude line]. But it was the section between Lake Superior and the start of the 49th parallel {the Manitoba/U.S.A. border}, especially that part of the border through the Lake of the Woods, which caused the most problems).

The Lake of the Woods showing Northwest Angle (could easily be invaded one weekend).

From Lake Superior the border went west through the Pigeon River and a succession of other rivers and lakes, to Fort Frances. It's a complicated border route and it caused a number of border disputes (the Americans wanted the border to go north from Thunder Bay to Dog Lake and Lac des Milles Lacs, and the British wanted the border to go south to Duluth). But once the fur trade stopped the border controversies stopped too (hardly anybody lived along this stretch of the border to keep the border disputes going).

From Fort Frances the border went west through the Rainy River to the Lake of the Woods. This section of the border didn't cause a lot of controversy though and there are a string of Canadian towns living along it (Fort Frances, Emo, Barwick, Stratton, Pinewood, Sleeman, Rainy River).

But then between the southern end of the Lake of the Woods and the 49th parallel there was a lot of controversy. After the American Revolution it was agreed that the border

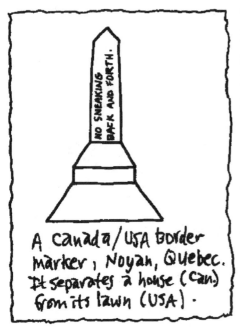

A canada/USA border
marker, Noyan, Quebec.
It separates a house (Can.)
from its lawn (USA).

would go through the Lake of the Woods to "its most northwestern part." But where was "its most northwestern part?" The Lake of the Woods is one of the most irregularly-shaped lakes you'll ever find anywhere.

It took Canada and the U.S.A. 90 years to agree on where this "most northwestern part" was. First they put it at Kenora. Then they put it in a swamp at the end of an inlet (1825). Then the boundary marker at this spot burned in a forest fire and was flooded when the lake's water level rose. Then they found that 2½ acres of this swamp was in Canada when it should have been in the U.S.A. Then Canada and the U.S.A. agreed that this area was really quite worthless, but they went ahead and drew the border to this northwestern part anyway (1875).

By that time the rest of the border west of the Lake of the Woods had already been set along the 49th parallel. The result was that a small peninsula of land sticking out into the lake north of the 49th parallel at this "most northwestern part," was left in the U.S.A. when it should have been in Canada. It's called the Northwest Angle of Minnesota.

The Northwest Angle of Minnesota is 130 square miles of swampy forest and one hamlet (Angle Inlet, Pop. 50). The border station is one small unmanned wooden video phone

booth with two buttons inside marked "Canada" and "U.S.A."
A little bit of Minnesota attached to Manitoba that should be in
Ontario. The only way in or out of it by land is through Canada. Quite a mess. A

The Sort of Agricultural Hand Implements Depicted as Walking Down Yonge Street, 1837.

border mistake. A small border mistake, but a border mistake
nonetheless. The Northwest Angle should be in Canada, but it's
not. Canada could trade a border mistake that's in Canada but
should be in the U.S.A. for it, but there are none to trade. All
the border mistakes are in favour of the U.S.A.

The War of 1812 may have been the last war fought in
Canada, but after that there were a couple of rebellions (small
civil wars), the odd insurrection or two, a few riots (including
one over a hockey player), a kidnapping and murder, and the
occasional pie thrown at a politician. But nothing major.

The rebellions were the rebellions of 1837 and 1838 in
Upper and Lower Canada. In Lower Canada there was rioting
and six battles in Montreal and the Richelieu River valley
before the rebels were defeated. Two hundred and ninety-eight
rebels and 27 Canadians/British were killed, 12 rebels were
hanged, 58 were transported to Australia, nine were transported
to Bermuda (it's a real punishment for a northern North
American to be sent to a warm climate), and the rest escaped to
the U.S.A.

The rebellion in Upper Canada was a little less dramatic.

(a) The Windmill Battle of the Windmill 1838.
(b) The Historic Site formerly a windmill formerly a lighthouse Near Prescott, Ontario

(a)   (b)

Some 600 rebels gathered at Montgomery's Tavern on Yonge Street in Toronto. (Montgomery's Tavern was on the west side of Yonge Street north of Eglinton at the present day location of Montgomery Avenue. In 1837 Montgomery's offered rebels and non-rebels alike, a public bar, ladies and escorts lounge, party room for hire, and an outdoor patio in the summer).

The rebels captured an alderman (who later shot a rebel, escaped, and became mayor of Toronto), marched down Yonge Street armed with a few rifles and agricultural hand implements, and were met by two dozen armed Canadians at Dundas Street. Two rebels and one Canadian were killed and the rebels fled. (One of those captured was John Montgomery of Montgomery's Tavern. He was sentenced to hang, told the judge he'd keep a tavern on Yonge Street once again, was pardoned, sentenced to transportation to Australia, jailed in Fort Henry, escaped from Fort Henry by tunnelling through a wall, stole a boat and took refuge in the U.S.A. He was eventually pardoned due to age, returned to Toronto and kept a tavern on Yonge Street once again).

Several days later more rebels were dispersed in Brantford, Ontario and from Montgomery's Tavern again. Three hundred rebels met at Montgomery's and marched down Yonge Street to St. Clair Avenue where they were met by 1,500

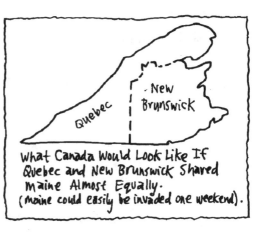

What Canada Would Look Like If Quebec and New Brunswick Shared Maine Almost Equally. (Maine could easily be invaded one weekend).

Canadian militia. One rebel was killed and Montgomery's Tavern was burned down (business was never the same in Montgomery's Tavern after that).

The rebels regrouped on Navy Island in the Niagara River where they declared the Republic of Canada, raised their own flag (blue and white bands with two silver stars) and were promptly dispersed again.

Rebel raids were also made on Pelee Island in Lake Erie (11 rebels killed); Dickinson's Landing, Ontario (one of the drowned villages near Morrisburg now under the St. Lawrence Seaway); Windsor, Ontario (25 rebels and four Canadians killed, 44 rebels captured, six hanged at London, Ontario, 18 transported to Tasmania (the coldest part of Australia) and 16 deported to the U.S.A.; and at Prescott, Ontario, where at the Battle of the Windmill (now a lighthouse and an historic site), 80 rebels and 16 Canadians were killed and 157 rebels arrested. The arrested rebels were tied to a rope single-file like kindergarten children on an outing and marched to Kingston and tried. Eleven were hanged, 60 were given all-expenses-paid-one-way-trips to sunny Australia (the most severe punishment

Famous Hats In
Canadian History

#4

Lower Canada
Militia 1813

they could think of after hanging), three died on their own and 85 were pardoned and never did it again.

It was the last armed conflict in Canada until the Fenian Raids (1866) and the Red River Rebellion (1870).

Canadians though were not just sitting around waiting for these next raids and rebellions to happen. They were out there exploring and settling into the empty spaces and building their country. After all, there were still a lot of empty spaces out there and up there to explore and settle into that nobody yet knew about.

Ontario and Quebec which used to be together as the Province of Quebec and were then separated into Upper Canada and Lower Canada, were united again into one province of two parts called the United Province of Canada, consisting of Canada West and Canada East. Their capital was Ottawa, chosen by Queen Victoria (1857) because they were not united as to which city their capital should be. So after 18 years and four different capitals (Quebec, Montreal, Toronto, Kingston) they asked Queen Victoria to choose a capital for them and she chose Ottawa; which Quebec, Montreal, Toronto and Kingston didn't agree with which is precisely why she chose it (Ottawa didn't really care if it was the capital or not and never really expected to be chosen).

The New Brunswick/Maine border is finally settled after 59 years, four treaties and the unsuccessful arbitration of the King of the Netherlands (they couldn't really ask Queen Vict-

oria to do everything).
The border wiggles around quite a bit in its eastern portion before settling onto a nice straight line based on the 45°N latitude line and heading directly west to the St. Lawrence River. But as with Alaska there is

"Tree Hanging Over Toronto Harbour." a drawing from a drawing by Elizabeth Simcoe 1793. (the tree later fell into the harbour).

a big border mistake here. It's not difficult to miss. Why does Maine stick so far up into Canada?

The New Brunswick/Maine border is the oldest part of the Canada/U.S.A. border. As Canada didn't exist then, all the negotiating for the north side of the border was done by Britain. They didn't try very hard. The Americans on the other hand were negotiating for themselves. So they tried very hard.

The New Brunswick/Maine border today follows the St. Croix River from its mouth to its source, before taking off in its characteristic loop north and ending up back on the 45°N latitude line where it started off. Along the west part of the Maine border and the tiny bit of the New Hampshire border, the border follows the high land dividing the rivers that flow north into the St. Lawrence (Canada), from the rivers that flow south into the Atlantic (U.S.A.).

But during the War of 1812 the British occupied Maine down to the Penobscot River (below 45°N). So the border could have been negotiated much further south than it is today.

However after the War of 1812 Britain and the U.S.A.

agreed to return to the borders that existed before the war started. Before the war started the border was the St. Croix River. But the two sides could not agree on which river was the St. Croix River.

To start with nobody seemed to use the name St. Croix any more. The Americans said the St. Croix River was really the Magaguadavic River (east of the St. Croix). The British said that the St. Croix River was really the Schoodic River, which was actually just another name for the St. Croix River (they should have said it was the Penobscot River).

To complicate matters further the maps they used to negotiate from showed two rivers in the vicinity of the St. Croix River (there are actually more than that). But which rivers were the rivers shown on the map and which of them (if any), was the St. Croix?

What ruined everything was that they eventually found a marker at the St. Croix River, so they had their starting point. They then had to figure out where the border went from there.

The British wanted the border to go north to the Aroostook River (south of the eventual border). The U.S.A. wanted it north of Lake Temiscouta, Quebec (north of the eventual border). They couldn't agree. So they called in the King of the Netherlands as an arbitrator and he put the border closer to the British claim than the American claim. But the Americans rejected this arbitration award as not being good enough, so they negotiated some more.

The border was finally settled somewhere between the American claim and the British claim, but closer to the British claim than the King of the Netherlands had it. So the Americans lost out a bit on that one. They should have gone with the King of the Netherlands' original award in the first place. However if the British had stuck to their strong bargaining position after the War of 1812 ended, then the New Brunswick/Maine border

The Sort of Wide-Brimmed Sun Hat Preferred by Elizabeth Simcoe for Drawing in.

could have looked much different today than it does.

The 45°N latitude line used for the Quebec/New York/Vermont section of the border could simply have been extended further east to the St. Croix River (once they found out where it was). That would have made things a lot simpler. And neater. But it didn't turn out that way. And so Maine sticks up into Canada just like Alaska hangs down into Canada. Where they shouldn't.

When the War of 1812 ended the British were in Fort Astoria (Oregon State), at the mouth of the Columbia River. The border was extended west along the 49°N latitude line (49th parallel) to the Rocky Mountains and Britain and the U.S.A. agreed to "share" everything else west to the Pacific. They called it the "Oregon Territory" (1818).

As part of this "sharing" of the Oregon Territory, Britain claimed everything south along the coast to 42°N (the current Oregon/California boundary) and the U.S.A. claimed everything north along the coast to 52°40'N (the current southern boundary of Alaska). But Britain then abandoned Astoria and the U.S.A. flooded settlers into the Oregon Territory using the "Oregon Trail." So when it came time to extend the border further west Britain proposed that it should simply be extended to the coast along the already established 49°N latitude line and the

Military Helmet Worn by "The Pig" in the Pig War 1860-1872. (courtesy: San Juan Island War Museum)

Americans happily agreed (1846). The U.S.A. really had no claim to any territory north of this line anyway and they had beaten the British to the "shared" territory south of it, so they were really quite pleased with this border arrangement.

Meanwhile north of the border the British formed the new colony of British Columbia and built Fort Victoria on Vancouver Island. They were worried that part of the island fell below 49°N and they wanted possession of all of it. What they did not want was another Northwest Angle situation on the west coast. However despite all their best intentions and efforts it didn't work out that way and the Canada/U.S.A. border got a British Columbia version of the Northwest Angle anyway. It's called Point Roberts.

The Americans may have lost their border claim that Oregon should stretch all the way north to Alaska, but they weren't overly worried. They later won the border dispute that Alaska should stretch all the way down the coast of British Columbia and they also won the dispute about where the border should go in the channel between Vancouver Island and the mainland.

On San Juan Island, just off Vancouver Island, there was a 12-year military standoff between Britain and the U.S.A. over who owned the island. They both claimed it. This standoff is known as "The Pig War" because the only casualty was a British pig that was shot by an American farmer after it strayed across onto the wrong side of the "border" (it was buried with full military honours).

As the two sides couldn't agree on who owned San Juan Island and where the border should go, they called in another arbitrator. The German Emperor Wilhelm I (Kaiser Wilhelm) this time, who promptly sided with the American claim (1872). And so the U.S.A. got most of the islands east of Victoria, B.C. and a little tip of land south of 49°N that is American, but attached to Canada: Point Roberts.

Point Roberts is 4.9 square miles of U.S.A. separated from Canada by a ditch and from the rest of the U.S.A. by 10 miles of water. It's another border mistake. Another Northwest Angle. The Northwest Angle of Washington State.

And so with that little territorial disagreement with Canada peacefully settled in their favour yet again, just like all the others, the U.S.A. turned its attention south and went off to war with Mexico.

Canadians though were not just sitting around after all this excitement and loss of border disputes waiting for 1867 and Canadian Confederation to come along. They were out there exploring and settling into the empty spaces and building their country. After all, there were still a lot of empty spaces out

Alex MacKenzie
from Canada
by land
22ᵈ July 1793

Painting on a Rock by Alexander Mackenzie,
Mouth of Bella Coola River, B.C., 1793.
First Graffitti on West Coast of Canada.

there and up there to explore and settle into that nobody yet knew about.

And the biggest empty spaces to explore that nobody yet knew about were in the Canadian Arctic. Especially the Canadian Arctic west of the empty spaces where James, Hudson, Frobisher, Davis, Baffin, Bylot and Foxe had been.

The Canadian Arctic is a frozen mass of frozen straits, frozen bays, frozen fiords, frozen inlets, frozen channels, frozen sounds, frozen gulfs, frozen passages, frozen islands, frozen peninsulas, frozen capes and bits of frozen ocean. Why anybody would want to explore there is a mystery. But they did. They wanted to explore there precisely because it was there to explore. A mystery. A blank spot on the map. Explorers love blank spots on the map. Unfortunately any blank spots left on the map today are quite small. A mountain top. A lake. But certainly nothing at all like the big blank spot on the map that the Canadian Arctic used to be.

They also wanted to explore the Canadian Arctic to

continue searching for "The Northwest Passage." The short cut to China. The Holy Grail of Canada. A water route from the Atlantic to the Pacific through the frozen Arctic that Frobisher, Davis, Baffin, Hudson, James, Bylot and Foxe had been looking for over 200 years earlier.

But they never found it this time either. Nobody found the Northwest Passage until

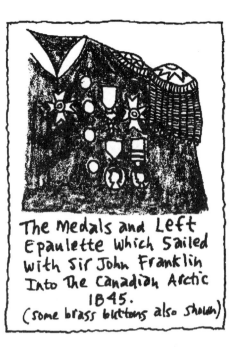

The medals and left epaulette which sailed with Sir John Franklin Into the Canadian Arctic 1845.
(some brass buttons also shown)

well after 1867. But still they tried. (However once they did find it they found that it really wasn't much good for anything after all. There were better, safer, warmer ways to get to China.)

SOME OF THE FRANKLIN RELICS FOUND BY JOHN RAE - 1854.

Fork   Spoon   Pusher

John Bell was in Fort McPherson in the Mackenzie River delta. Instead of going north along the Mackenzie River which had already been done, he went further west and found the Porcupine River which flowed into the Yukon River which flowed into the Pacific. Captain James Cook followed the west coast around the Aleutian Islands to the top of Alaska.

buffalo steaks

buffalo burger

buffalo ribs ↓

head ↓

buffalo rug →

buffalo pie or chip ↓

leg warmers →

beard ↑

ANATOMY OF A BUFFALO OR BISON.

Frederick William Beechy (Cape Beechy) went a bit further.

But most of the Canadian Arctic explorers approached from the east: William Barrow (Barrow Strait), John Ross (Ross Point), Edward Parry (Parry Islands), Joseph Banks (Banks Island), Thomas Simpson (Simpson Strait), Peter Warren Dease (Dease Strait), John Rae (Rae Strait), Joseph Rene Bellot (Bellot Strait), Edward Belcher (Belcher Channel) and John Franklin (Franklin Strait).

John Franklin discovered a lot of coastline and land in the Canadian Arctic as well as frozen ocean and became Sir John Franklin. But he is best known for getting lost.

As a result of Sir John Franklin getting lost in the Canadian Arctic, at least two dozen people led expeditions out looking for him or for clues to his whereabouts, including, well after 1867, people from the University of Alberta. Sir John Franklin contributed more to Arctic exploration than anybody, simply by getting lost.

James Ross went looking for him, but found the Magnetic North Pole instead. Richard Collinson and Robert McClure went looking for him, but got lost themselves and had to be rescued by people who went out looking for them while at the same time looking for

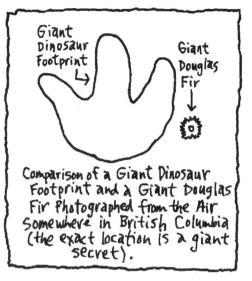

Giant Dinosaur Footprint ↳

Giant Douglas Fir ↓

Comparison of a Giant Dinosaur Footprint and a Giant Douglas Fir Photographed from the Air Somewhere in British Columbia (the exact location is a giant secret).

Franklin. John Rae went looking for him, found evidence of the Franklin expedition and claimed the reward (other people found bits and pieces of the Franklin expedition but got no reward except articles in *National Geographic* magazine).

Also as a result of Sir John Franklin getting lost in the Canadian Arctic, a picture was painted in 1851 showing "The Arctic Council Planning a Search for Sir John Franklin." Ten men, most of whom were also Arctic explorers, are shown around a table at British Admiralty headquarters poring over charts. Two are seated and eight are standing. On the wall behind them is a large portrait of Franklin.

Unfortunately the Arctic Council never existed and the meeting was never held. Sir John Franklin also contributed to Canadian fictional art simply by getting lost.

Canada certainly had a lot of empty spaces to explore, get lost in and poke around in. And because the empty spaces to poke around in were much bigger than the unempty spaces that had already been poked around in, people were always

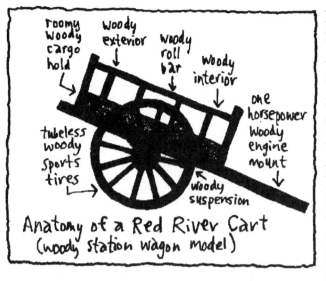

roomy woody cargo hold

woody exterior

woody roll bar

woody interior

one horsepower woody engine mount

tubeless woody sports tires

woody suspension

Anatomy of a Red River Cart
(woody station wagon model)

poking around in them.

Abraham Gesner was a family doctor in Nova Scotia who also liked poking around in the ground. He poked around in the ground along a river bank in New Brunswick one day and found a thick, gummy oil. He distilled it and was the first to produce kerosene (earlier he had been the first to produce paraffin/coal oil from coal). Gesner's process to make kerosene also produced a volatile and at the time unwanted by-product called gasoline. It would be the search for oil to produce Gesner's kerosene though that would kick-start the Oil Revolution.

James Miller Williams of Hamilton, Ontario, was poking around in the ground near Oil Springs, Ontario, when he found oil (1857). It was the world's first commercial oil well.

The Industrial Revolution began in England and was fuelled by coal. It ended and was replaced by the Oil Revolution. The Oil Revolution began in Oil Springs and Petrolia, Ontario, Canada and was fuelled by oil. We're still in it. The Oil Revolution hasn't been replaced by anything yet. Oilmen from Canada were the first to poke into the ground all over the world for oil, and the first to develop oil well

VOL. I   DAWSON N.W.T. APRIL 1ST 1898   NO. I

THERE'S NO GOLD HERE!
HONEST.
NO FOOLIN'.

Failed Headline for the First Issue of The Klondike News, April 1, 1898.

technology too (the Americans were preoccupied with their Civil War and in finding oil for themselves at this time).

People were poking around in the ground in the Fraser and Thompson River valleys of British Columbia when they found gold (1858). Two years later they found gold further north in the Cariboo River District of British Columbia. Two years after that they found gold further north in the Stikine River District of British Columbia. Thirty-four years after that they found gold further north in the Klondike River District of the Yukon Territory. In fact they formed the Yukon Territory because of it (1898).

So heading into the year 1867 the country which would later become Canada was comprised of: five colonies in the east

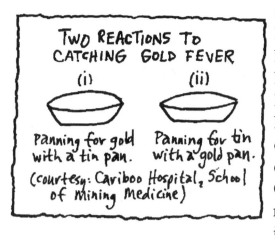

Two Reactions To
Catching Gold Fever

(i)   (ii)

Panning for gold   Panning for tin
with a tin pan.   with a gold pan.
(courtesy: Cariboo Hospital School
of Mining Medicine)

called the United Province of Canada, New Brunswick, Nova Scotia, Prince Edward Island and Newfoundland. One colony out west called the Red River Colony, which looked rather small all by itself out on its own in the middle of the continent but which was actually almost twice as big as the United Kingdom, and over twice as big as Nova Scotia, New Brunswick and P.E.I. combined (it extended down into the U.S.A. too). One colony really out on its own on the west coast called British Columbia. And a whole, great, big, huge area called Rupert's Land (which nobody still knew how big it was), filling in all the blank spaces in between. Rupert's Land was still shown as a blank spot on the map. But it was still considerably larger than all the non-blank spots on the map of Canada put together.

They fished, cut trees, made boats and farmed in the eastern colonies. They cut trees, made boats, farmed, trapped furs and brewed beer in the Province of Canada ("Good ale is all I want" -- John Molson, Montreal, 1786. "I fancy I should like brewing better than anything" -- John Labatt, London, Ontario, 1847).

They trapped furs and buffalo, made pemmican, tried to farm and shot at each other in the Red River Colony. And they fished, cut trees, made boats, traded furs and looked for gold on the west coast.

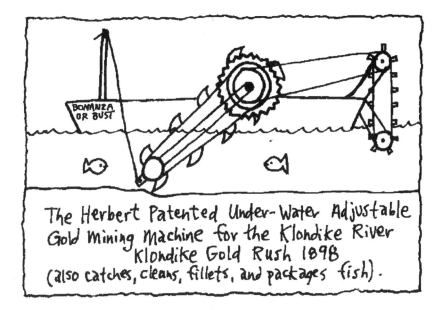

The Herbert Patented Under-Water Adjustable
Gold Mining Machine for the Klondike River
Klondike Gold Rush 1898
(also catches, cleans, fillets, and packages fish).

But one of the problems with people poking around in the wide open spaces of Canada before 1867, was that if they ever died out there but wanted to be buried back where they came from, it could be a difficult job granting their last wish.

John Rowland worked for the Hudson's Bay Company and died at Fort Pitt in 1854 (near Lloydminster, Saskatchewan/Alberta). He was a big man (they called him "Big Mountain") and in his will he stated that "my bones should rest in Montreal" (1,800 miles east). His wish was fulfilled by the Hudson's Bay Company.

They buried him at Fort Pitt in 1854, dug him up in the spring of 1855, boiled the flesh off the bones, put the bones in a barrel of rum and took the barrel to Winnipeg by canoe (1,350 miles), where it spent the winter of 1855.

In the spring of 1856 the barrel went north by York boat to York Factory on Hudson's Bay (1,050 miles), where it spent the winter of 1856.

HOW NOT TO GET TO THE KLONDIKE
The Klondike Whisky Barrel Roller Wagon
3 large whisky barrels, iron axles, wood frame
(fell apart near St. Albert, Alberta 1898).

In the spring of 1857 the barrel went east by ship to London, England (7,600 miles) and then west to Liverpool (195 miles) where it spent the winter of 1857.

In the spring of 1858 the barrel went west to Montreal (6,500 miles) where the barrel was opened and the bones of John Rowland were put to rest. Exactly as he'd wanted. Four years and 16,700 miles later. (If he'd said "my body should rest in Montreal" instead of "my bones," it's doubtful even the Hudson's Bay Company could have done it.)

Sophia Cameron died in Barkerville in the Cariboo District of British Columbia in 1862. Her husband was John "Cariboo" Cameron, who later struck it rich in the Cariboo along with Billy Barker, "Dutch" Bill Dietz, "Doc" Keighley and "Twelve-Foot" Davis. She wanted to be buried in their home town of Lancaster, Ontario (near Cornwall, 2,250 miles east). Her wish was fulfilled by Cariboo Cameron.

They put her in a wood coffin lined with tin, put the coffin on a toboggan, and John Cameron and some friends dragged it 400 miles through deep snow to Harrison Lake.

There it was put on a boat to Victoria (200 miles), where the coffin was filled with alcohol, re-sealed and buried in 1863. John Cameron then returned to the Cariboo, struck it rich, got the nickname "Cariboo," and packed away

The Main Gate, Fort Providence N.W.T. 1850
(it was too fancy to use everyday so everybody just used the back gate).

enough gold to pay to transport his wife further east. In the winter of 1863 he returned to Victoria, dug up Sophia, put the coffin on a ship to San Francisco, another ship to Panama, the railway across the Isthmus of Panama, a ship to New York and the railway to Lancaster, Ontario, where Sophia Cameron was buried in December. As she'd wanted. Fourteen months and 8,000 miles later.

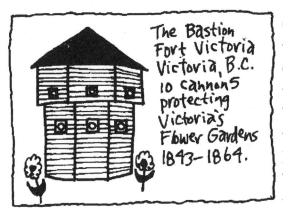

The Bastion Fort Victoria Victoria, B.C. 10 cannons protecting Victoria's Flower Gardens 1843-1864.

Unfortunately Cariboo Cameron then returned to the Cariboo, died, and was buried there. There was nobody to transport him back to Lancaster, Ontario to be buried with his wife.

CHAPTER SEVEN

After 1867. Just shortly After 1867

Ship York Boat Canoe Iceberg Sealskin Inner Tube

Early Hudson Bay Transportation
(courtesy: York Factory Rapid Transit Corp.)

And so 1864 came along and then 1866 (two pretty important dates) and then 1867 (the really important date, although perhaps not as important as all that); and then before you knew it it was 1868 and already after 1867 (time flies quickly when you're a new country).

Actually quite a lot happens in a very short time just shortly after 1867 in the new Dominion of Canada. Some more provinces want to join Canada, and some still don't. The Fenians are raiding again. The Americans look like they might poach the entire Canadian west. There are railways to be built. There is one new government formed that doesn't last very long, and one small rebellion that lasts a very long time. It is a rebellion which is held in two different parts, with two different names and 16 years between the parts; but it is still basically the same rebellion. Canada's borders with the U.S.A. are being settled. Canada gets some new territory, but loses the chance to get some more. The Arctic is still there to explore. Canadians invent time zones and the telephone.

Canada just shortly after 1867 is not a quiet country at all. In fact it's a very busy place indeed. And most of the action is in the Canadian West, which is only fair since most of the action before 1867 was in the Canadian East.

In 1867 Thomas Spence owned a store in Portage la Prairie, Manitoba (except it wasn't called Manitoba then it was still called Rupert's Land owned by the Hudson's Bay Company). But Thomas Spence thought it was a good idea that Rupert's Land should join Canada. So he wrote a note on birch bark to the Prince of Wales inviting him to come and visit Portage. When the invitation was not accepted Spence decided to form his own government: the Government of Manitobah (Thomas Spence was not a good speller).

So in 1868 Thomas Spence was elected the first President of the new Government of Manitobah. He drew out large boundaries for his new state, informed the Colonial Office of the new government, and began collecting taxes. So far so

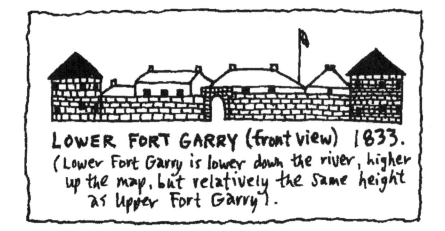

LOWER FORT GARRY (front view) 1833.
(Lower Fort Garry is lower down the river, higher
up the map, but relatively the same height
as Upper Fort Garry).

good. But that was the easy part.

The Hudson's Bay Company refused to pay taxes on its own land. And a local shoemaker named MacPherson accused the new government of using the tax money collected to buy liquor for Spence and his new council. Spence had MacPherson arrested, but at the trial MacPherson not only defended himself well and won the case, he discredited Spence and his new government. The first self-declared Government of Manitobah collapsed in a heap of humiliation. The next self-declared government in Manitoba however, did not go nearly so quickly or so quietly.

In 1869 the Hudson's Bay Company sold Rupert's Land to Canada for £300,000 and 45,000 acres of land scattered all over Western Canada. The area was renamed the Northwest Territories, or the North West Territories, or the North-West Territories (lots of people at that time were not good or consistent spellers), and Ottawa sent the first lieutenant-governor of the new territories, "Wandering Willie" MacDougall, to the Red River Colony.

But the Métis living there (half French or English-half

Indian), do not want Wandering Willie wandering into their territory. So they form a committee with Louis Riel as secretary and try to stop Wandering Willie from

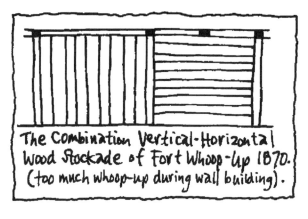

The Combination Vertical-Horizontal Wood Stockade of Fort Whoop-Up 1870. (too much whoop-up during wall building).

wandering in. But Wandering Willie wanders in anyway. So the Métis form a new self-declared government with Louis Riel as President and Thomas Spence helping out and with their own army and their own flag (blue fleur-de-lis on white background). Then they march in and capture Fort Garry, hold 48 prisoners, and escort Wandering Willie back to the U.S.A. border (at that time the quickest way from Toronto to Winnipeg was through the U.S.A.).

Next the new government seizes all the guns and ammunition it can get their hands on, shuts down the Red River newspaper, and gives it to an American to run who favours the American takeover of Canada. Not a nice state of affairs. Not the sort of thing you would expect to happen in a quiet country. This is actually quite a lot of excitement happening all at once in the new Dominion of Canada just two years after Confederation. But it's not all that's happening.

A trading post called Fort Whoop-Up is opened in Lethbridge, Alberta by American whisky traders. Things are getting out of control in the Canadian West. Because of this Newfoundland decides not to join Confederation. It was never like this before 1867. Before 1867 there were conferences and meetings and balls and paintings and photographs and things were peaceful and civilized. There was none of this armed rebellion and whooping-it-up business going on. But it's not over yet. The excitement just keeps on continuing and a lot happens in 1870 too.

In 1870 Louis Riel has one of the 48 prisoners in Fort Garry executed and the rebellion gets an official name: The Red River Rebellion.

An Early N.W.M.P. Truncheon.

Prince Edward Island decides not to join Confederation either. They like peace and quiet, law and order and good government too. But British Columbia wants to join Canada (they're used to a wild lifestyle out there), and Manitoba really wants to join Canada to get out of the mess they're in.

So Manitoba becomes Canada's fifth province (1870). It doesn't start off as a very big province though. It's only a little square province and people laugh at it and call it the "Postage Stamp Province" even though it's over seven times bigger than P.E.I. (but less than one-sixteenth its eventual size).

As Manitoba is now an official part of Canada, the Prime Minister sends an official armed force to the Red River to restore law and order, good government and the quiet life. But when they get there they find that Fort Garry is empty and Louis Riel and the rebels have fled to the U.S.A. It's a letdown, but the Red River Rebellion is over. It's only the first part of the Red River Rebellion though, Red River Rebellion Part I.

As if that isn't enough excitement however, the Fenians

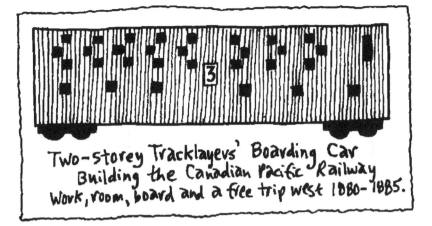
Two-storey Tracklayers' Boarding Car
Building the Canadian Pacific Railway
Work, room, board and a free trip west 1880-1885.

start raiding again. They raid into southern Quebec, but are beaten back at Eccles Hill (1870, three Fenians killed). The next year they raid into southern Manitoba in support of Louis Riel and the Métis, but are escorted back across the border by American troops (they still don't have any permission from Washington to invade).

After 1870 is over though, things quieten down a bit and Canada offers railways to P.E.I. and British Columbia to tempt them into joining Confederation. B.C. jumps at the chance and becomes Canada's sixth province (1871). But P.E.I. is still playing hard to get. They build their own railway and still don't join Canada.

Canada now stretches from sea to sea, but with a large, unorganized blank spot on the map called the Northwest Territories in the middle.

Surprisingly the boundaries of British Columbia are not all that difficult to draw up. The boundary through the mountains was set in 1858 when B.C. first became a colony, and is based on encompassing all that territory where the rivers flowed west. Likewise the northeast and northern boundaries

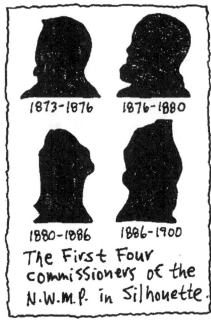

1873-1876   1876-1880

1880-1886   1886-1900

The First Four
commissioners of the
N.W.M.P. in Silhouette.

use convenient straight longitude and latitude lines based on keeping all west- and south-flowing rivers (and their gold-mining areas), within the province. The border with Alaska however becomes a sticky situation, but not for some time yet (see Chapter 2).

Canada grants a charter to the Canadian Pacific Railway Company to build a railway to the Pacific coast in ten years, and the Inter-colonial Railway between Montreal and Halifax is completed (1876).

The railway that Prince Edward Island built itself however, is deep in debt. And so in 1873, six years late, P.E.I. swallows its pride and becomes Canada's seventh province ("among the people who thronged the streets there was no enthusiasm"). Indeed, when the official Confederation document is read from Province House in Charlottetown "the audience consisted of three persons, and even they did not appear to be very attentive".

Since the Prime Minister now has a mounted force out in the northwest with nothing much to do (the Red River Rebellion rebels ran away), he forms them into the North West Mounted Police for the Northwest Territories; and Canadians would forever from that time onward have difficulty remembering what is the correct spelling for Northwest: North West, North-

A Red River Freighter's Boat 1858
(adapts to a Red River Cart at the
flick of a switch).

West, or Northwest?

Because of this the new police force becomes known as the NWMP, and the new territories the NWT. Later on the NWMP are renamed the RCMP (Royal Canadian Mounted Police); and the Northwest Territories, formed at the same time as the Province of Manitoba, officially becomes the Northwest Territories, with no alternative spelling permitted.

One of the first things the NWMP do is march west, close down Fort Whoop-Up, and open up new police stations along the way. In 94 days 1,200 soldiers trek 1,000 miles through land where hardly anybody has been before and not many people live. They get as far as Fort Macleod and Fort Edmonton, Alberta. The march becomes known as "The Great Trek West of 1874," and it is recreated 125 years later as a means of selling RCMP T-shirts and mugs.

At the same time as the NWMP are trekking west, surveyors are building stone cairns, earth mounds and wood markers along the 49th parallel to mark the Canada/U.S.A. border.

Then, just as things had quietened down nicely in Western Canada, Louis Riel pops up again in Manitoba even

The Sort of Decorative chest Bulls-Eye Target Worn by Chief Poundmaker in the Northwest Rebellion, 1885.

though the Prime Minister paid him $1,000 to stay away. He is elected to Parliament, unexpectedly shows up in Ottawa, dashes into the House of Commons, takes the oath, signs his name, and dashes out again to Hull, Quebec before they can catch him (he is wanted for murder in Ontario).

Because Louis Riel does not attend the House of Commons he is expelled. He is then re-elected and expelled again. Then he is committed to a Montreal mental hospital and becomes an American citizen (the two events are not connected).

With Louis Riel out of the way again for awhile, Canada gets back to the business of being a quiet country. It tries to attract new immigrants, but finds it has a bad reputation in Europe (people do not always tell the truth about the climate in Canada or the level of cultural sophistication in the NWT), and so the U.S.A. gets more immigrants than Canada does.

The Canadian Arctic is still there to explore and Britain gives Canada all the rest of it that it doesn't already have (1880), even though nobody really knows yet how big it is, what's been given away, and what's been received.

A British naval ship reaches Floeberg Beach on Ellesmere Island in the Canadian Arctic, rents a cottage on the ocean for a week and sets a record for the highest altitude ever reached by a ship: 82°N (1875). The next year another British ship gets to 83°20'N. Then an American ship gets to 83°24'N (1881-83). But of course what everybody really wants to do is to get to the North Pole first (they don't do it until 1909).

Tired of being called "The Postage Stamp Province," Manitoba's boundaries are extended three more times before it reaches its final shape (1881, 1884, 1912). It then calls itself "The Keystone Province" and people stop laughing at it.

Husky the Musky
Largest Fish Ever
Caught in The Lake
of the Woods.
Stuffed and mounted
in Kenora.

As part of the settling of the Manitoba/Ontario boundary, there is a dispute over who owns the area between the current boundary and Thunder Bay, especially the town of Rat Portage (Kenora, Ontario). Ontario wins.

With Manitoba now removed from the Northwest Territories as a separate province, the rest of the Northwest Territories is divided up into districts (Athabasca, Alberta, Saskatchewan, Assiniboia, Keewatin), with the leftover part remaining as the NWT (the huge part that nobody really knows how big it is).

It's now 1885. Things have quietened down nicely in Canada. Louis Riel hasn't caused a rebellion for 16 years and hasn't been thrown out of the House of Commons for 11 years. Then Louis Riel returns to Canada. He sets up another government at Batoche, Saskatchewan (the Métis have now moved further west out of Manitoba), and declares independence from Canada. Treason! Guilty of trying to set up a new country within a new country. For the second time. The North West Rebellion has begun (or the North-West Rebellion

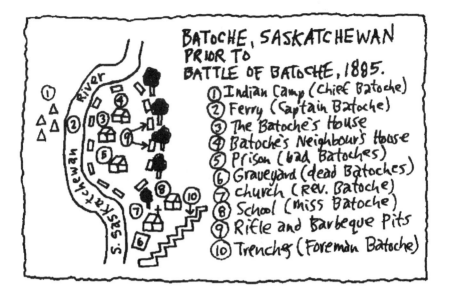

BATOCHE, SASKATCHEWAN PRIOR TO BATTLE OF BATOCHE, 1885.
① Indian Camp (Chief Batoche)
② Ferry (Captain Batoche)
③ The Batoche's House
④ Batoche's Neighbour's House
⑤ Prison (bad Batoches)
⑥ Graveyard (dead Batoches)
⑦ Church (Rev. Batoche)
⑧ School (Miss Batoche)
⑨ Rifle and Barbeque Pits
⑩ Trenches (Foreman Batoche)

or the Northwest Rebellion). It is really just a continuation of the Red River Rebellion though, Red River Rebellion Part II, except it takes place in Saskatchewan this time, not Manitoba, and lots of Indians join the fighting as well as the Métis.

There are incidents and engagements at places with animal names: Duck Lake, Frog Lake, Fish Creek, Loon Lake. And there are incidents and engagements at places without animal names: Battleford, Cut Knife, Frenchman Butte, Fort Pitt, Batoche. Altogether 71 rebels and Indians and 46 Canadians are killed.

But this rebellion does not last very long. Canada has the new NWMP all mounted and ready to go (they are good at marching and trekking by now), and although the CPR railway is not totally complete yet, the railway company carries more troops out west and transports them overland between the gaps in the railway line. So Canada is able to get a big army out there quite quickly.

Fifty-four days after declaring independence, the rebellion ends at Batoche. Fifty-seven days after declaring independence, Louis Riel is captured. Two hundred and forty-two days after declaring independence, Louis Riel is hanged for treason.

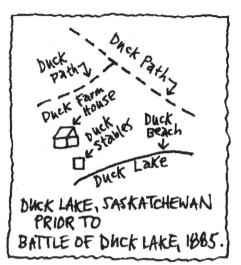

DUCK LAKE, SASKATCHEWAN PRIOR TO BATTLE OF DUCK LAKE, 1885.

With Louis Riel gone from the scene there is no more armed fighting in Canada ever again. No more invasions, raids, insurrections, or rebellions. Just the odd cream pie, milk jug, or rotten tomato thrown at a politician.

And so Canada settles down to becoming the quietest, second-biggest country in the world. Alexander Graham Bell invents the telephone in Brantford, Ontario (1874) so quietly that the Americans later claim that he invented it in the U.S.A. even though Bell himself says he invented it in Brantford, and if anybody ought to know where they were when they invented the telephone, then you'd think that the one who invented it would know, wouldn't you?

FISH CREEK, SASKATCHEWAN PRIOR TO BATTLE OF FISH CREEK, 1885.

Richard Harris completes the original first painting of the

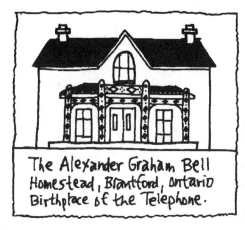

The Alexander Graham Bell Homestead, Brantford, Ontario Birthplace of the Telephone.

Fathers of Confederation (1883, it had 34 Fathers of Confederation in it), the one that was destroyed by fire when the Parliament Buildings burned down in 1916 and was repainted by Rex Woods in 1965. This is the famous Fathers of Confederation painting we have now that a lot of Canadians think depicts the Fathers of Confederation in Charlottetown in 1867, but which really depicts a combination of the Fathers of Confederation in Charlottetown in 1864 and the Fathers of Confederation in Quebec in 1864, in Quebec City.

The last spike in the last rail completing the CPR railway is driven in by the President of the Bank of Montreal at Craigellachie, British Columbia (1885), and the famous "Last Spike" photograph is taken. (Everyone is wearing a hat and dark clothes. Only Donald Smith, the bank president wielding the hammer, and Sandford Fleming, chief engineer of the CPR and inventor of the time zones standing behind Smith, have snowy white beards and add a touch of white to an otherwise dark and gloomy black and white photograph.)

CHAPTER EIGHT

After 1867.
Up to 55 years after 1867

The boundaries of British Columbia, Canada's sixth province, have existed as they are now since 1866; far ahead of Manitoba the fifth province obtaining its final shape (1912), and even before Ontario and Quebec, two of the four original 1867 provinces, obtained their final shapes (also 1912).

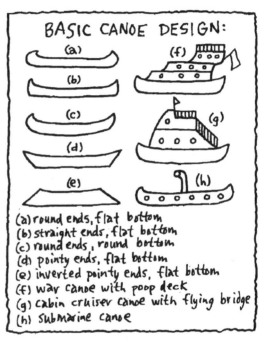

BASIC CANOE DESIGN:

(a) round ends, flat bottom
(b) straight ends, flat bottom
(c) round ends, round bottom
(d) pointy ends, flat bottom
(e) inverted pointy ends, flat bottom
(f) war canoe with poop deck
(g) cabin cruiser canoe with flying bridge
(h) submarine canoe

In fact it was because of British Columbia that Alberta, Saskatchewan, Manitoba, Ontario and Quebec all obtained their final shapes. If it wasn't for B.C. the insides of Canada would not look like they do today. For creating a lot of the internal provincial boundaries of Canada, we owe it all to B.C.

The northern boundary of British Columbia was set at 60°N latitude. The eastern boundary was the line running through the mountains. When they came to fill in the area

ESKIMO FEMALE FACE TATOOS

The Aivillik
Paddle-Cheeks
and half-Goatee

The Nechillik
Whiskers and
Full-Goatee

between B.C. and Manitoba with the two new provinces of Alberta and Saskatchewan (1905), all they had to do was to divide up the remaining area roughly equally using nice straight longitude lines.

Because British Columbia already went north to 60°N, Alberta, Saskatchewan and Manitoba all wanted to be extended north to 60°N too. So they were.

Because British Columbia, Alberta, Saskatchewan and Manitoba all extended north to 60°N, Ontario wanted to be extended north to Hudson's Bay and Quebec wanted to be extended north to the Ungava Peninsula. So they were. It was British Columbia that was responsible for all this extending north of the other five provinces to the east.

The Yukon Territory got its final shape in 1898. But the Northwest Territories (1870) were gradually being pushed north as other provinces were carved out of its territory (Manitoba, Saskatchewan, Alberta). Its final boundaries (1908) were set as everything east of the Yukon as far east as you could go (Baffin Island); and everything north of 60°N as far north as you could go (the North Pole).

So by 1912 the internal map of the Dominion of Canada was almost complete (minus Newfoundland and Labrador and Nunavut). The second-biggest country in the world had basically been put together. Alberta would be as far west from Newfoundland as Germany was as far east. Vancouver would be closer to Mexico City than it was to Halifax, Nova Scotia. And St. John's, Newfoundland would be closer to Ireland than it was to Winnipeg.

Canada was a country of territories and provinces. Not states. This seems a simple enough thing to understand. Yet people are forever trying to give Canada states.

Prince Edward Island

Anticosti Island

Vancouver Island

A Comparison of Islands (guess which one is a province).

The U.S.A. has states. Australia has states. Brazil has states. South Africa has states. But Canada has provinces. New Zealand has provinces too (small ones) and so does Argentina. Britain has provinces, but they are not official provinces, they are counties that are sometimes called provinces. So having provinces is not an unusual thing. Canada has official provinces, but somehow people are always wanting to call them states.

A province is defined as: "A division of an empire or nation, or the countryside or small city contrasted with a big city". Having provinces therefore suits Canada very well. Canada is a nation that at one time used to be part of an empire, and Canada certainly has the contrast between the countryside or small city and a big city.

There are ten provinces and three territories in Canada, and each one has its own big city. Some of them have more than one. The only thing that varies is the size of their bigness.

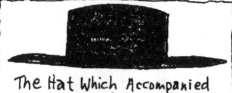

The Hat Which Accompanied
Roald Amundsen Through The
Northwest Passage 1903-1906.
(the ear-muffs are tucked-up inside).

The ten provinces of Canada come in various sizes of bigness too. The largest province, Quebec, is the size of the UK, France, Spain, Portugal, Belgium, Holland and Luxembourg put together. Or Texas, two Californias and a Maryland.

The smallest province, Prince Edward Island, is just over two Luxembourgs big. Or 1.8 Rhode Islands. The other eight provinces fall in size somewhere between these two.

But 40% of Canada is not divided into provinces at all, but territories. The Yukon Territory is smaller than Alberta, Saskatchewan or Manitoba; and just slightly smaller than France or California and Alabama combined.

The Northwest Territories, despite the fact that 60% of it was whittled away to form the new territory of Nunavut (1999), is still the same size as France, the UK, Germany, Portugal, Ireland, Denmark and half a Luxembourg; or about the same size as Texas, California and a Nevada.

The new territory of Nunavut though is now the biggest jurisdictional area in Canada. More than one-fifth of Canada is in Nunavut. It's the same size as France, the UK, Germany, Italy, Spain, Ireland and 2½ Luxembourgs; and bigger than Alaska with California included. The territories of Canada may be short on people, but they sure don't skimp on land area.

Exploration in the Canadian Arctic continued. Nobody yet knew just how big it was. It was still a blank spot on the map. And explorers love blank spots on the map. They still

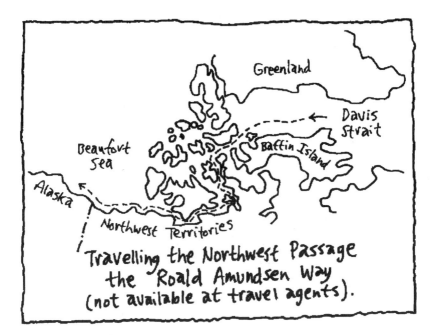

Travelling the Northwest Passage the Roald Amundsen Way (not available at travel agents).

hadn't found the Northwest Passage. And they still hadn't been to the North Pole.

Roald Amundsen (Norway) finds the Northwest Passage from the Atlantic Ocean to the Pacific Ocean through the Arctic Ocean after spending three winters frozen in ice (1906). His route was: Davis Strait to Bylot Island, turn left; Lancaster Sound to the Parry Channel, turn left into Peel Sound between Somerset Island and Prince of Wales Island; down the west coast of the Boothia Peninsula and through James Ross Strait; around King William Island, through Storis Passage and into Queen Maud Gulf (sounds more exotic than it is); follow the channel south of Victoria Island through Dease Strait, Coronation Gulf and Dolphin and Union Strait to Amundsen Gulf. It's now clear sailing past the Mackenzie River delta along the north shore of Alaska to the Bering Strait and the

Pacific Ocean. But has it all been worth it? Not really. Not many people make the trip after Amundsen.

Another Norwegian, Otto Sverdrup, discovers the Sverdrup Islands (1902). Tired of Norwegians sailing around and discovering its Arctic, Canada annexes all of the Arctic islands that it didn't already have, regardless of who discovered them (1908).

Shortly after Amundsen finds the Northwest Passage, Robert E. Peary of the U.S. Navy becomes the first person to reach the North Pole (1909). Was it worth it? Must be. People still keep on trying to reach the North Pole today. (The first person to reach the North Pole was Santa Claus. But if you live there full-time and travel in and out once a year using a flying sleigh, then that doesn't really count as being an explorer.)

At the North Pole there is a barber pole painted in red and white swirls with a sign saying "North Pole" attached to it. When you reach the North Pole the tradition is to plant your flag in the snow next to the pole, have your picture taken leaning on it (posing for an oil painting at the North Pole is not done very often as the paint tends to congeal quickly at polar temperatures), and carve your initials into it. (Although Santa Claus lives close to the North Pole he does not appreciate visitors, and explorers are asked not to bother looking for him. Mailbag deliveries at Christmas time are always left beside the pole for pickup by Santa's Little Helpers when no one else is about.)

Canadians though were not just sitting around letting other people discover its Arctic, its Northwest Passage and its North Pole. They were out there exploring and settling into all the other empty spaces and building their country. There were still a lot of empty spaces out there to explore and settle into.

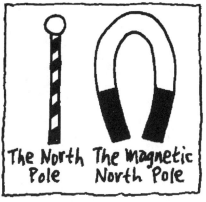

The North Pole   The magnetic North Pole

The first trans-Canada train goes from Montreal to Port Moody, British Columbia. Gold was found in the Yukon and 300,000 prospectors rushed north to the Klondike to pay $18 for a dozen eggs. Canadians formed the Yukon Territory; wrote *Anne of Green Gables*; built the world's largest lift-lock; invented Marquis wheat, basketball and five-pin bowling; and played the first-ever Grey Cup game. (The cup couldn't be presented the first year because it hadn't been finished yet. But it was presented for the first time at the second Grey Cup game.)

The fairly new country of Canada had its provinces, territories, trains, Grey Cup, and Arctic explored (they now had a pretty good idea of how big it was). All that was left to do now was to adopt a national anthem and a flag.

The Klondike Reversible Jacket Eaton's Catalogue 1896 (for gold miners).

The Klondike Gold Rush Nightshirt with Roll Collar and Storm Cuffs. Eaton's Catalogue 1896. (one size fits all, comes with tent pegs and guy ropes).

The song "O Canada" comes from Quebec. The music was written in bilingual notes by Calixa Lavallée, with words in French by Adolphe Routhier. It was first performed by three bands and a choir of 3,000 in Quebec City in 1880.

Quite a number of English versions of the words were written, but the one that came to be accepted was written by Stanley Weir, a judge and author of legal works and verse (1908).

However in 1967 the Government of Canada changed some of the English words in the Canadian national anthem (but not the French words). Why? Why did they not stand on guard over the national anthem? The Canadian national anthem was only 59 years old before it was tampered with.

The Dutch national anthem is the oldest national anthem in the world and one of the best (words written in 1568, music in 1629). In it are two lines pledging a now long-outdated allegiance to the King of Spain. But did the Dutch government change the words to their national anthem? Never. They've stood on guard over the original words for their national anthem for more than 400 years. Why? Because it's part of their history.

The First Note of the Dutch National Anthem. (from piano score)

In 1982 the Government of Canada changed Dominion Day to Canada Day. Why? Would the U.S.A. change Independence Day to America Day? The government of Canada is not very good at standing on guard over Canada's history. But these are only temporary modern-day failings by temporary

Some Failed Designs for a New Canadian Flag.

The "Captain Canada" Flag.

The "Sir Sandford Fleming" Flag.

"Pearson's" Pennant

The "Sea to Shining Sea" Flag.

modern-day Canadian governments. They can easily be changed back again by another future Canadian government as determined to preserve Canadian history as the Canadian governments of 1967 and 1982 were to change it.

The Canadian flag though was a much more difficult thing to come up with than the national anthem. And it took a lot longer to do too (the Canadian government did this one as well). It was 98 years after Confederation that Canada got its red maple leaf flag. It was not an amalgamation of several old flags into one new flag. It was not a flag left over from history. It was not a flag that was still there in the morning with bombs bursting in air. It was nothing so grand or romantic as that.

It was not the Red Ensign. It was not even the Canadian Red Ensign (combination of the British Red Ensign with the

Canadian coat-of-arms which had been the unofficial official flag of Canada since 1945).

It was the Canadian red maple leaf flag (red maple leaf on white background with red bars on each side). A flag born and bred in Ottawa by the government of Canada. It was a government project. A product of a government flag committee. A flag chosen by the government of Canada. A flag not chosen by the people of Canada. They never had a vote on it (they never voted to have the words in the national anthem changed, or Dominion Day changed to Canada Day either).

The flag of Canada was voted on by the Parliament of Canada in 1965. The only debate was whether the bars on each side of the red maple leaf would be red or blue, or whether the maple leaf in the middle would be one red maple leaf or three red maple leafs on a red stem (maple leafs are only blue on hockey sweaters). There was really no debate that the symbol in the middle of the flag would not be a maple leaf (the maple leaf easily beat out the beaver).

The government and the Prime Minister wanted the red bands. The opposition party wanted the blue bands. But there was never any doubt that the flag the government and the Prime Minister wanted would be the flag that Canada got. And it was.

What was surprising however, was that for a flag delivered by government, the red maple leaf Canadian flag didn't turn out to be such a bad flag, did it? It could have been a lot worse. It could have turned out like the Newfoundland flag. But it didn't. It turned out to be a flag that was attractive, symbolic, distinctive, easily recognizable and simple enough to be drawn by kindergarten children. Everything a good flag should be.

CHAPTER NINE

After 1867. From just over 55 years after 1867 until now

This is where we are now. Compared to before 1867 hardly any time at all. Compared to before 1867, just shortly before 1867, 1867 itself, and up to about 45 years after 1867; not as exciting a time either (Canada had really settled down to being a bonafide quiet country by this time).

Most people think that after 1867 Canada was an independent country. Well it was, and it

How To FIND THE ST· PIERRE and MIQUELON ISLANDS FROM OTHER WELL- KNOWN ISLANDS.

Newfoundland.

N.S.

① From the Magdalen Islands.
② From St. Paul Island.
③ From Brunette Island.
④ From Merashpen Island.
⑤ From Great Colinet Island.

wasn't. There were still some areas of the British North America Act of 1867 that needed to be sorted out. Mainly complicated legal things. These were not actually done until 1931 (Statute of Westminster, Canada becomes a truly independent country), and 1982 (Canada Act/Constitution Act,

Newfoundland and Labrador - A province of triangles and arrows.

Canada gets a whole new bunch of complicated legal things like a Constitution and a Charter of Rights and Freedoms).

Newfoundland and Labrador became Canada's tenth province in 1949. It had taken 82 years after Confederation for Newfoundland and Labrador to finally decide to join Canada. It was the best offer they'd had (it was the only offer they'd had, they were bankrupt). Greenland didn't invite them to become part of Denmark. The St. Pierre and Miquelon Islands didn't invite them to become part of France. The United Kingdom didn't invite them to become part of the United Kingdom. Europe didn't invite them to become part of Europe. The U.S.A. didn't invite them to become part of the U.S.A. So they joined Canada instead.

Newfoundland and Labrador brought to Canada folk music, cod-jigging, Screech and icebergs. And the Labrador-Quebec boundary dispute.

Like the British Columbia, Yukon and New Brunswick boundaries the Labrador/Quebec boundary is based upon where rivers flow. But this boundary took a lot of twists and turns to get to where it is today.

The Labrador/Quebec boundary is the longest inter-provincial boundary in Canada (over 3,500 km long). But it has not yet been surveyed and marked on the ground. It exists only as marks on a map. It is a half-finished, semi-permanent, permanent boundary.

At one time the colony of Newfoundland contained not only the island of Newfoundland, but the "Coasts of L a b r a d o r , " Anticosti Island and the Magdalen Islands as well (1763).

Anticosti Island
a drawing from a drawing from
a drawing by Elizabeth Simcoe.

Then everything except the island of Newfoundland was transferred to Canada/Quebec (1774). Then Newfoundland got Labrador and Anticosti Island back (1809). Then they lost Anticosti Island and the south coast of Labrador to Canada/Quebec again.

After 1867 when Canada became a country and Quebec became a province, Quebec protested Newfoundland granting timber licences in Labrador (1902). Quebec asked Ottawa to submit the Labrador/Quebec boundary dispute to the Judicial Committee of the Privy Council in England. They did (1904). But nothing happened (privy councils are part of government and governments take a lot of time to do things).

Eighteen years later nothing much had happened still, so Canada and Newfoundland asked the Privy Council again to define the Canada/Newfoundland border in Labrador (1922). Five years later (lightning speed for a privy council), the Privy Council found in Newfoundland's favour and set the boundary in its present location based on watersheds and the height of land.

When Newfoundland and Labrador joined Confederation in 1949, the Labrador/Quebec boundary was confirmed in the "Terms of Union." In 1971 a Quebec royal commission looked

What the Canadian Arctic Islands Would Look Like Floating off the Coast of Western Europe.

into the Labrador/Quebec boundary question, but decided that Quebec really had no case (royal commissions are part of government too, and take almost as much time to do things as privy councils). And there the Labrador/Quebec boundary sits. On the map. Waiting to get onto the ground.

The next big internal jurisdictional change in Canada was the creation of the new territory of Nunavut in 1999. This was done by taking away yet more land from the Northwest Territories. The NWT had shrunk again. From being Rupert's Land that was so big nobody knew just how big it was, the NWT had been withered away to a Northwest Township less than 1/10th the size of the continent of Antarctica, less than 1/5th the size of the continent of Australia, and less than ½ the size of the sub-continent of India. A sorry state of affairs (however the NWT is still over 535 times bigger than Luxembourg).

At the moment then there are no plans for any new provinces or territories in Canada. But you never know. In 1974, 1987 and 2004 the Turks and Caicos Islands in the

Caribbean asked to become a new territory of Canada, but were turned down by Ottawa. Again, as with the flag, the national anthem and Dominion Day, the people of Canada never had a say in the matter. If they had then they probably would have

Some of the Turks and Caicos Islands (the rest are so small you need a microscope to see them).

voted for the Turks and Caicos Islands becoming a part of Canada. And why not? Canada's own winter vacation spot. No passports required. Direct flights. The U.S.A. has the U.S. Virgin Islands. France has Guadeloupe and Martinique. Holland has the Netherlands Antilles. The UK has Caribbean islands. Why couldn't Canada have the Turks and Caicos Islands? No reason whatsoever (the government of Canada has a lot to answer for).

If there were to be any new province in Canada, other than the territories becoming provinces or Labrador becoming a separate province; then the obvious choice is the creation of the new Province of Northern Ontario.

Ontario has the most noticeable north-south divide in it of any province in Canada other than Newfoundland and Labrador. Ontario has a great big northern part of its province attached to a little southern part by a narrow gooseneck of land between Georgian Bay and Quebec (French River, Lake

The Remains of a Labrador Whale Flipper Pie with Chips and Coleslaw. (courtesy: Belle Isle Café)

Nipissing, Mattawa River). To the north of this line is Northern Ontario. To the south Southern Ontario. And they are two quite different Ontarios, separated by geography and distance (and in Northwestern Ontario by a time zone).

If Prince Edward Island can be a province, and Nunavut can be a new territory, then anything is possible. There is no reason Northern Ontario couldn't one day be its own province (if Northern Ontario were a province it would be 168 times bigger than P.E.I.).

But other than Newfoundland and Labrador entering Confederation 82 years late, Nunavut being created and the possibility of the new territory of The Turks and Caicos Islands and the new province of Northern Ontario; modern Canadian history isn't overly exciting. Certainly nothing like the big excitements of ancient Canadian history before 1867, in 1867 and just shortly after 1867.

In modern Canadian history there's just little bits of small excitements popping up here and there every now and again. The last Father of Confederation dies. Newfoundland sends out the first trans-Atlantic flight and receives the world's first radio signal. There's a strike in Winnipeg; a riot, kidnapping and murder in Quebec; and Indian insurrections and deaths in Ontario and Quebec. The Calgary Stampede, the Bluenose and the Dionne Quintuplets are launched. Canadians invent the plug-in radio, Pablum and snowmobiles; beat Russia

What Northern Ontario Would Look Like As A Province Compared To The Maritime Provinces.

at hockey; write "*In Flanders Fields*"; and discover oil in Alberta and insulin in Ontario. Just little bits of small excitements (which is why most Canadian history books fill up the modern Canadian history sections with economics, politics and politicians).

But what more could you expect? After 1885 Canada had settled down to become the quietest, second-biggest country in the world. It had its borders, boundaries, provinces, territories, flag, national anthem, curling and hockey; what more did it need?

Canada had become one of the world's great quiet countries. Not such a bad thing to be though is it? After all there are far too many noisy countries in the world already.

A Collection of Odes Done in the Limerick Style and Inspired by Canadian History

"The Matthew" Finds Newfoundland 1497. First Discovery of North America Since the Vikings.

Ode to the Matthew

There once was a ship called the Matthew,
    That sailed from Bristol all brand-new.
It found New Founde Lande,
    Which everyone thought grand,
So it filled up with fish and said "thank you!"

Ode to John Cabot

There once was an explorer
named Cabot,
With a name that sounded
something like "rabbit."
"I beat Columbus, you know,
But history doth show,
That I just didn't go round and
blab it!"

The Sort of Flexible Explorer's Cap/ Toque/Nightcap Favoured by John Cabot 1497. (bobble optional)

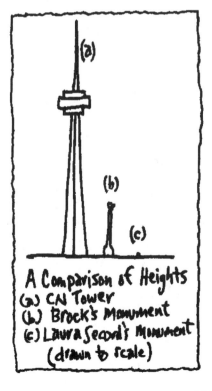

A Comparison of Heights
(a) CN Tower
(b) Brock's Monument
(c) Laura Secord's Monument
(drawn to scale)

Ode to General Brock

There once was a General
named Brock
Who was a chip off the old
General's block.
But he charged up the hill,
As brave Generals will,
And was shot by a waiting
flintlock.

Laura Second's House
Queenston.

Chocolates not
sold here.
My other house
is in Chippawa.

Ode to Laura Secord

There once was a lady quite small,
　　Who did a war deed exceedingly tall.
She walked 19 miles,
　　But came up all smiles,
For she helped the Americans fall.

Ode to Lord Selkirk

There once was a tall Scottish lord,
　　Who spent more than he could afford.
But he built the Colony Red River,
　　Despite winters of shiver,
And died without seeing the reward.

Ode to John Rowland

There once was a barrel of rum,
That contained the bones of a chum.
It was put on a ship,
For a very long trip,
And buried with a successful outcome.

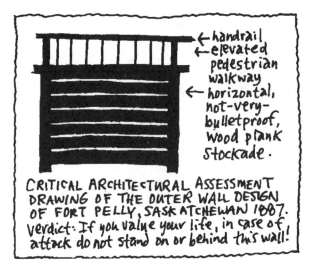

← handrail
← elevated
pedestrian
walkway
← horizontal,
not-very-
bulletproof,
wood plank
stockade.

CRITICAL ARCHITECTURAL ASSESSMENT
DRAWING OF THE OUTER WALL DESIGN
OF FORT PELLY, SASKATCHEWAN 1887.
Verdict: If you value your life, in case of
attack do not stand on or behind this wall!

Ode to the NWMP March West

There once was a march that marched west.
For 93 days without rest.
They found Whoop-Up Fort,
That sold whisky and port,
But there was nobody there to arrest.

Ode to the John Franklin Expedition

There once was a sled in the snow,
So loaded down it barely could go.
It carried stoves and spittoons,
And knives, forks and spoons,
And an 800-pound bateau.

The Ruffled Variety of Scarf Favoured by Henry Hudson for Exploring the Canadian Arctic – 1610. (starched white)

Ode to John McCrae

There once was a Surgeon Commander
Who said: "That's enough, Faderlanders."
So he stayed in the mud,
With the bodies and blood,
And wrote a poem about poppies in Flanders.

Collage of Inkblot's favourites that almost didn't make the book

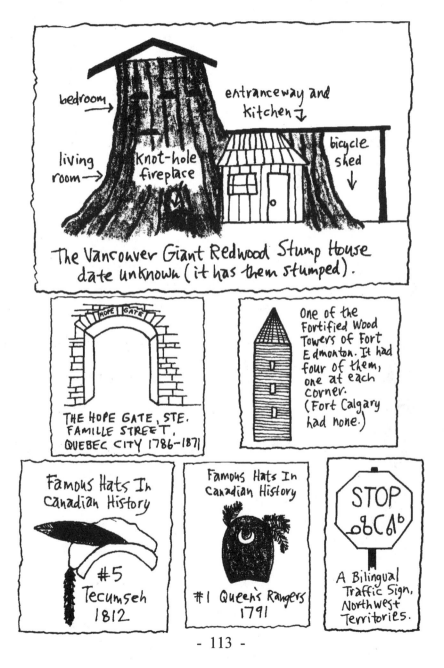

bedroom →

entranceway and kitchen ↴

living room →

Knot-hole fireplace ↓

bicycle shed ↓

The Vancouver Giant Redwood Stump House date unknown (it has them stumped).

HOPE GATE

THE HOPE GATE, STE. FAMILLE STREET, QUEBEC CITY 1786-1871

One of the Fortified Wood Towers of Fort Edmonton. It had four of them, one at each corner. (Fort Calgary had none.)

Famous Hats In Canadian History

#5 Tecumseh 1812

Famous Hats In Canadian History

#1 Queen's Rangers 1791

STOP

A Bilingual Traffic Sign, Northwest Territories.

More of Inkblot's favourites

Percé Rock
Gaspé
Québec.
As seen
while
floating
on an
air mattress
in the
horizontal
lying down
position.
WARNING:
Don't get
too close
to the
mouth! ←

Famous Hats In Canadian History

#2 General Wolfe 1759

The Sort of Pointy Nose Normally Attributed to General Wolfe.

Famous Hats In Canadian History

#3 General Burgoyne 1776.

Famous Hats In Canadian History

#6 Northwest Rebellion 1885.

Famous Hats In Canadian History

#7 Boer War 1899

Even more of Inkblot's favourites

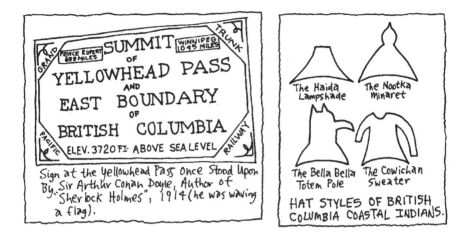

SUMMIT OF YELLOWHEAD PASS AND EAST BOUNDARY OF BRITISH COLUMBIA ELEV. 3720 FT. ABOVE SEA LEVEL

GRAND TRUNK PACIFIC RAILWAY

PRINCE RUPERT 699 MILES   WINNIPEG 1095 MILES

Sign at the Yellowhead Pass Once Stood Upon By Sir Arthur Conan Doyle, Author of "Sherlock Holmes", 1914 (he was waving a flag).

The Haida Lampshade   The Nootka Minaret

The Bella Bella Totem Pole   The Cowichan Sweater

HAT STYLES OF BRITISH COLUMBIA COASTAL INDIANS.

The Alberta Hotel, Edmonton 1888
Stopover on the Klondike Gold Rush
Longest bar in Alberta
Watering-hole of Bob Edwards of
"the Calgary Eye Opener"

STRAW GAS

The Alternative Energy Car
University of Saskatchewan 1919
(it failed as a land vehicle, but flew
around the world in eighty days).

Still more of Inkblot's favourites

The Hudson's Bay Company White Depot Building
All That Remains of York Factory, Manitoba
(13 windows across and 10 windows deep).

HOW TO MAKE AN INDIAN MOCCASIN

1. Get Piece of Leather
2. Cut into Moccasin Shapes
3. Sew into Moccasin (add lace)
4. Decorate to Taste or Tribe Tradition.

The Bottom End of the First Escalator in Canada Eaton's, Toronto, 1910.

The Nose Ornaments Worn by Chief Atlin, Medicine man, Nootka, Vancouver Island 1904.

CANADA
FREE HOMES FOR MILLIONS
GOD BLESS THE ROYAL FAMILY

Part of the Canadian Coronation Arch
London, England 1902
(It was 56 feet high, 60 feet wide, and decorated like a wedding cake.)

The last bunch of Inkblot's favourites that almost didn't make the book

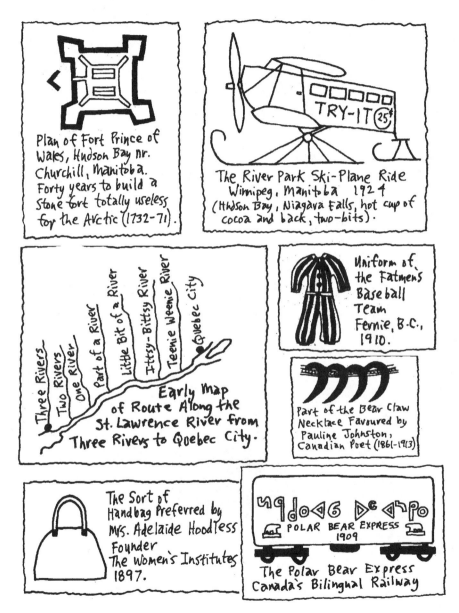

Plan of Fort Prince of Wales, Hudson Bay nr. Churchill, Manitoba. Forty years to build a stone fort totally useless for the Arctic (1732-71).

The River Park Ski-Plane Ride Winnipeg, Manitoba 1924 (Hudson Bay, Niagara Falls, hot cup of cocoa and back, two-bits).

TRY-IT 25¢

Three Rivers Two Rivers One River Part of a River Little Bit of a River Ittsy-Bittsy River Teenie Weenie River Quebec City

Early Map of Route Along the St. Lawrence River from Three Rivers to Quebec City.

Uniform of the Fatmens Baseball Team Fernie, B.C., 1910.

Part of the Bear Claw Necklace Favoured by Pauline Johnston, Canadian Poet (1861-1913)

The Sort of Handbag Preferred by Mrs. Adelaide Hoodless Founder The Women's Institutes 1897.

POLAR BEAR EXPRESS 1909

The Polar Bear Express Canada's Bilingual Railway

About the Author

Geoffrey Corfield lives in Canada. In fact he was born here. In the hospital on South Street just down from the Victoria Tavern. It used to be called Victoria Hospital. It's now called South Street Hospital. The Victoria Tavern however is still called The Victoria Tavern. God Save The Queen.

Geoffrey Corfield has lived in three provinces and worked in four, curls, drinks Waterloo Dark, knew Max Bentley, but has never wanted to be Prime Minister or go to the North Pole.

He writes **INKBLOT**, a weekly Canadian humour column: 500 words, one limerick, once a week since 1993; and produces **INKBLOT** postcards. This is his fourth book. South Street is a one-way street.

Also by Geoffrey Corfield:

Any or all of these fun and educational books are available from **DESPUB**, 2340B Clifton St., Allanburg ON L0S 1A0, or despub@niagara.com or toll-free, 1-866-471-4123.

Free shipping and handling and a 30% discount is offered with orders of five books or more of any of our titles . . . and miniature Hershey bars are always included with every shipment.

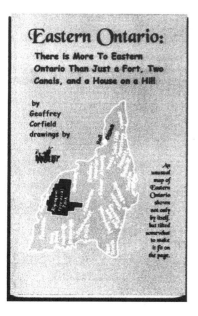

MEMBER OF SCABRINI GROUP

Québec, Canada
2007